WORK AND THE WORK ETHIC
IN AMERICAN DRAMA, 1920–1970

Work and the Work Ethic
in American Drama
1920-1970

THOMAS ALLEN GREENFIELD

UNIVERSITY OF MISSOURI PRESS

COLUMBIA & LONDON, 1982

Library of Congress Cataloging in Publication Data

Greenfield, Thomas Allen, 1948–
Work and the work ethic in
American drama, 1920–1970.

Bibliography: p. 179
1. American drama—20th century—History
and criticism.   2. Work in literature.   3. Work
ethic in literature.   I. Title.
PS338.W65G7   812'.5'09355   82–4909
ISBN 0–8262–0374–4   AACR2

DEDICATED TO
J. D. SPRAGUE

ACKNOWLEDGMENTS

I am grateful for the tireless efforts of Professor J. D. Hurrell of the University of Minnesota, whose sound judgment and generous encouragement were essential to the completion of the work. I am also grateful for the assistance of Professors G. T. Wright, Robert Moore, Hyman Berman, and Archie Leyasmeyer of the University of Minnesota. Their support and guidance helped make the writing of this work a most pleasurable and valuable experience.

I extend here, as I have elsewhere, my thanks to the United Negro College Fund, whose financial assistance during academic years 1977–1978 and 1978–1979 allowed me to complete my research and writing. The securing of these critical funds would not have been possible without the efforts of Dr. Allix B. James, President Emeritus of Virginia Union University, and Dr. Dorothy N. Cowling, Director of Federal Programs at Virginia Union University, as well as those of Dr. Bruce Welch and Professor Ruby T. Bryant, also of Virginia Union.

My research has been greatly assisted by the kind cooperation of Mrs. Verdelle Bradley and staff of the William Clark Library at Virginia Union University; Eileen Meagher, Janet Howell, and Elizabeth Brewer of the Inter-Library Loan division of the James Cabell Library at the Virginia Commonwealth University; and the staff of the Boatwright Library at the University of Richmond. In addition, I have received much-needed, perhaps too-much-needed, editorial assistance and advice from my typists, Ms. Christine M. Knight and Ms. Joy Payne.

I am deeply thankful to Alice Hermoine Rogstad for agreeing to be a writer's spouse for two years; I look forward to returning the favor in the near future.

Finally, I wish to express my thanks to my daughter, Suzanne Margaret Rogstad Greenfield, who spent the first nineteen months of her life as my constant companion in the research and writing of this book.

T. A. G.
Richmond, Va.
May 1982

CONTENTS

INTRODUCTION

A thematic study of a body of literature is, by necessity, a parasite. It can exist only after the completion and widespread dissemination of earlier studies that have named and evaluated the major authors, detailed the historical background, and ordered the chronology of the relevant works at hand. Furthermore, a thematic study is likely to offend its "host" by wreaking havoc on established background material as it seeks to make literary "connections" that often transcend familiar considerations of time and place. Yet, like all parasites, it cannot afford to do such violence as to disable its host entirely; for the sake of its own survival it must accept certain limitations laid down for it by the studies that preceded it.

American dramatic literature from 1920 to the present has benefited from a plentiful if not exhaustive number of useful "hosts." Works such as Joseph Wood Krutch's *American Drama Since 1918* and Gerald Weales's *American Drama Since World War II* have established for us the major names, plays, and the important historical and literary background of American drama of the past sixty years. The material in these studies has been fleshed out rather fully by the most popular form of publication in the field: the extensive study of a single author, such as Louis Scheaffer's *O'Neill: Son and Playwright*, or a single play, such as Walter Meserve's *Studies in Death of a Salesman*.

Far less numerous are thematic studies in modern American drama. Although such studies do exist, they tend to reject the entirety of modern American drama as their scope in favor of one that is either narrower or broader. One often finds, for example, studies of themes or ideas that emerge in the American drama of certain decades, such as Morgan Himelstein's *Drama Was a Weapon* (radical drama of the 1930s) or C. W. E. Bigsby's *Confrontation and Commitment* (drama from 1959 to 1966). On the other hand, we also find books that discuss themes and ideas in all of modern drama, of which American drama is only a part and a rather small part at that. John Styan's *The Dark Comedy* and Robert Brustein's *The Theater of Revolt* are examples of such studies. What are far less numerous are full-length studies of themes and ideas that run through the entire period of modern American drama: studies that seek out the occurrence and recurrence of conflicts, problems, and philosophies that bind American dramatists to one another and comprise *en masse* a national dramatic literature. Both the possibility and the need for such studies are suggested by Jane F. Bonin's *Major Themes in Prize-Winning Drama*, in which she demonstrates that among plays that have won any of the Pulitzer, Obie, Critics Circle, and Tony awards, one finds recurrences of themes surrounding women, marriage, work, war, politics, and religion. One does find an occasional full-length study of a single theme, either in all of modern American drama or at least in several plays, such as Thomas Porter's *Myth and Modern American Drama*. But by and large, the criticism of modern American drama is rather finely chopped up into tiny parcels.

We need not spend much time defending the value of thematic analyses of literature. Thematic examinations of other literary periods and/or genres, such as E. M. W. Tillyard's *The Elizabethan World Picture* and Leslie Fiedler's *Love and Death in the American Novel*, have added immeasurably to our understanding and admiration of Renaissance drama and American fiction. Such studies have made us aware that a body of well-crafted, intelligently conceived literature eventually reveals to us a collective consciousness of men and society that is greater than the sum of ideas offered by the major writers of a given period or genre.

While I would not claim that modern American drama is nearly as rich in content as Renaissance drama or American fiction, it is sufficiently well established that we may take on the task of examining fully the themes, ideas, and philosophies that make up the American dramatists' collective statement on their own times. If literature is an important and valid reflection of people and their times, then certainly such a collective statement does as much to identify a body of literature as does the chronological history of that literature.

Of the several themes that recur in the sixty years of modern American drama, perhaps the most prevalent and most intriguing is the one surrounding the American and his work, involving conflicts that occur "on the job" and problems that arise in his attitude toward work itself.[1] Certainly the kinetic economic and social forces that mark twentieth-century American history—including the development of scientific management, the expansion of industrialism, massive immigration, the depression, the rise of the labor movement, and the growth of the American middle class—have served as important sources of inspiration for those American playwrights intent on dramatizing the impact that American society has upon the people who inhabit it. But a surprising number of plays about modern work also reflect "pre-modern," Puritan values toward work—values that frequently do as much to engage the dramatist's interest in work as does contemporary economic history. In fact, tensions between America's traditional Puritan attitudes toward work and America's modern attitudes toward work form the basis of conflict in many important modern American plays.

America's Puritan values regarding work and money, conventionally called the "work ethic" or the "Protestant work ethic," stem from the religious and economic history of the Reformation. It is a complicated phenomenon that merits some historical background here. According to

Max Weber's *The Protestant Ethic and the Spirit of Capitalism,* the work ethic evolved when Methodists, Calvinists, and Pietists sought to balance the weighty responsibilities of eternal salvation and worldly wealth.[2] What eventually emerged as seventeenth-century Puritanism was a philosophy of asceticism—a code of behavior for both wealthy capitalist and lowly worker:

> Truly what is preached is not simply a means of making one's way in the world but a peculiar ethic. The infraction of its rules is treated not as foolishness but as forgetfulness of duty. That is the essence of the matter. It is not mere business astuteness . . . it is an ethos.[3]

The now familiar homiletic virtues associated with that ethos—sobriety, frugality, "a cool self-control," and a belief in hard work as a virtue in and of itself—became the working philosophy of what C. Wright Mills describes as "a type of man capable of ceaseless methodical labor," a type of man whose social development is both justified and encouraged by the protestant sects that spawned him.[4]

But while his various personality traits or characteristics form the popular (and some have argued distorted) contemporary view of the Puritan, the Puritan character has not, in the view of many historians, had a major impact upon the development of Western capitalism. Daniel Rodgers and Herbert Gutman (as well as Weber) have observed that Puritanism introduced into Western society the process of systematically controlling one's environment, particularly one's economic environment. They contend that the major impact of Puritanism is rooted in this process. This process of rationalization gradually became the sustaining force of capitalist theory and practice from the eighteenth century to the present. Weber observes that the Protestant Reformation, far from being the liberating movement it is often portrayed to be, was, in fact, "a new form of control over the previous one [involving] a regulation of the whole of conduct, which penetrating to all departments of private and public life, was infinitely burdensome and earnestly enforced."[5] To the considerable extent that this new order embraced economics, it did so in order to rationalize, or to break down into manageable organizations and systems, all means of production, including human labor. Writing in *The Journal of Interdisciplinary History*, Daniel T. Rodgers argues that it is this rationalization of production and labor that brought Europe out of its traditional subsistence economy, with its static organization centered on kinship and village relations, and into its modern state of technical innovation with organized systems of labor and production. So strong is the Puritan's drive to rationalize and control his environment that it is possible to see the history of modern technological capitalism as ever more effective efforts on the part of capitalists to render production and labor into ever-increasingly systemized and rationalized systems, over which capitalists exercise ever larger amounts of control. This trend has evolved from the earliest removal of work and business from the household, to the formation of the nineteenth-century company town, to the introduction of scientific management theories into early twentieth-century industry, to the swelling of white-collar bureaucracies in modern corporations.[6]

Certainly in the evolution of modern American capitalism, the secular acquisitiveness of the Puritan looms larger than does his piety. Weber observes:

> The capitalist system so needs this devotion to the calling of making money, it is an attitude toward material goods so well suited to that system, so intimately bound up with the conditions of survival in the economic struggle for existence, that there can today no longer be any question of a necessary connection of that acquisitive manner of life with any single Weltanschaung. In fact it no longer needs the support of any religious forces and feels the attempts of religion to influence economic life, in so far as they can still be felt at all, to be much an unjustified interference as is regulation by the state.[7]

Rodgers confirms this notion, stating that it was precisely this desire for rational control over the environment, rather than religious fervor, that formed the basis for the hard-edged Puritan view of the American "wilderness":

> . . . the settlers of Puritan New England and Quaker Pennsylvania came with no hopes for prelapsarian ease. They were straighteners of crooked places, engaged in a task filled with hardship, deprivation, and toil. They did not expect to pluck treasures from the land but planned to civilize and tame it, even as they expected to tame the wild places in themselves. . . . Out of the American Eden they fashioned a land pre-occupied with toil.[8]

By the time Benjamin Franklin writes in the middle eighteenth century of frugality, punctuality, and self-mastery, he has given to traditional Puritan values "their most unambiguous secular expression."[9] To the average American at the dawn of the industrial age, the values of work are seen in terms of their utilitarian practicality rather than their godliness.

With its emphasis on a lifetime commitment to work, its measurement of man's character on the basis of how well he lived up to that commitment, and its promise of survival or even prosperity for the individual who applied himself diligently to his daily task, the work ethic was a guiding force in early nineteenth-century America, when most Americans were self-employed, worked in their own homes, and were engaged in either farm or craft work. "Men," Mills observes, "lived the legend of the self reliant individual." The penniless beginner did, indeed, work as a journeyman, save his money, learn his trade, and then hire another penniless beginner who continued the cycle. This system operated under what Adam Smith referred to as "the Guiding Hand"—a self-balancing society held together by countless free, individual transactions.[10] The promise of earning one's way to an independent farm, shop, or craft business was not only a reasonable ambition in early nineteenth-century America but was the primary ambition. The hardworking American was no myth but a reality.

However, the rise of American industrialism in the mid-nineteenth century, with its large factories, routinized work systems, and elaborate divisions of labor, not only altered the economic structure of America's self-employed economy but also altered significantly the work attitudes and values of the American worker. As America moved from a nation of self-employed individuals (80 percent in 1800) to a nation of employees (67 percent in 1870 and 80 percent in 1940), the commitment of the American to his work and his working life decreased in its intensity, and what some historians see as "a loosening of the work ethic" developed in response to the changing nature of work.

The reasons offered by social historians for this dissolution of traditional work values in modern, industrial America vary, but among the most commonly held views is the theory that once an individual no longer sells what he produces, that is, no longer owns his own shop or farm, but merely sells his labor to another (that is, to an employer) he becomes alienated from his work. This alienation is intensified as the process of division of labor becomes increasingly elaborate and removes the worker ever further from the end product of his labor. Harry Braverman, a most enthusiastic advocate of this theory, sees the advancement of modern industry in nineteenth- and twentieth-century America as an assault upon the independence of the American worker and, therefore, the value of his work: "Every step in the labor process is divorced so far as possible from precise knowledge and training and reduced to simple labor."[11] David Montgomery observes that from its earliest stages the division of labor in mills and factories was aimed at attacking the autonomy of the skilled craftsmen who had been hired by factories in the early nineteenth century and who maintained a measure of autonomy from their bosses, and a commensurate commitment to their work, as long as they knew more about their task than did their foremen or supervisors.[12] In an apparently conscious effort to gain control of labor and to systematize it, factories eliminated from most labor the "human dimension of work" by moving planning, scheduling, and other mental tasks off the factory floor and into the manager's office.[13] As Rodgers observes, these developments constituted a serious assault on the work ethic: "Part of what gave labor its immense value to the keepers of the mid-nineteenth century ethic was the assumption that the worker owned his own toil—that a man's efforts were his to exert and the successes his to be reaped."[14]

Another explanation offered by historians for the apparent abandonment of the work ethic in nineteenth-century America is that the onset of large-scale rationalized, systemized factory work in America created a conflict between traditional and modern attitudes of time on the part of American workers. The irregular hours of traditional task-oriented labor conflicted with the more rigidly ordered systems of modern factory work, which runs on time-oriented labor. The craftsmen and the farmer of pre-industrial America performed their tasks on a schedule required by the tasks themselves. Nature (which guided the chores in farm work) or the irregular and often unpredictable flow of trade marked an era in America that was like the pre-industrial eras in other countries—an era marked by extreme bouts of intense labor followed by intense idleness. But as succeeding generations of craftsmen and farmers entered the factories, it became the deliberate and conscious task of the mid-nineteenth-century factory managers to teach task-oriented workers to regulate their lives according to the time-oriented demands of daily shift work. Indeed, as E. P. Thompson has observed, the succeeding generations of task-oriented workers adjusted to the new time-oriented work routines of modern America so successfully that they eventually turned their new knowledge to their own advantage in their negotiations with managers:

> The first generation of factory workers were taught the importance of time; the second generation formed their short-time committees in the ten-hour day [movement]; the third generation struck for overtime and time and a half.[15]

The same effort that modern industry exerted in its attempt to convert nineteenth-century farmers and artisans from their premodern work habits to modern industrial time-oriented routines was sustained and intensified in late nineteenth- and early twentieth-century American industries, as mills and factories contended with an influx of immigrant peasants whose work habits and cultural backgrounds were at least as far removed from the systematic, rationalized modern industrial "round of life" as were those of the first generation of factory workers in America.[16] Noting the success of management efforts to alter these premodern habits through piecework and other production inducements, Gutman observes that the continuous flow of immigrants and migrants into the American work force from 1843 to the early twentieth century kept the composition of the American working class in a continuous state of flux. This instability, he argues, undermined long-standing, traditional work attitudes and work habits that gave rise to and sustained the Protestant work ethic in pre-industrial America.[17] The net effect, then, of this move from a traditional "round of life" to a modern "round of life" is, we are told, the demolition of the work ethic as a meaningful belief in the lives of the modern American working class:

> Industrialism upset the certainty that hard work brought economic success. . . . No amount of work by the semi-skilled laborer caught in the anonymity of the factory would open the way to self-employment or wealth. . . . As industrialization shook the idea of the permanence of

scarcity, it became harder and harder to insist that compulsive activity, work, and usefulness were the highest goals in life.[18]

In modern, industrial America, not only does the factory worker experience a loss of traditional work values, but, according to such historians as Mills and David Riesman, so does the modern white-collar worker. In *White Collar*, Mills argues that it is the very process of rationalizing the blue-collar work force—the process of dividing and breaking down human labor into sections and subsections of labor routines—that gave rise to a burgeoning class of bureaucrats in modern industry shortly after 1900. Their now all-too-familiar obsession with the manipulation of personalities, rather than with the enhancement of production, served to alienate them from the value of their own work, since their labor, too, was and is removed from their own control and their own initiative:

> By rationalizing the organization via rotation systems and control sections, top bureaucrats can guide the vision of underlings. The entrepreneural type who does not play ball can be excluded from inside information. Like the commodity market before it, the top level of the personality market may well become an object to be administered rather than a play of free forces of crafty, wild and unexampled initiative.[19]

So rapid and so thorough was the division and subdivision of labor among white-collar jobs that by 1920 pay and status advantages of white-collar workers over blue-collar workers virtually disappear.[20] With the devaluation of the clerical skills and accounting skills of the early white-collar worker comes a corresponding alienation from his work and an abandonment of traditional work attitudes:

> Neither the protestant view of work as religious fulfillment nor the Renaissance view of the craftsman controlling the work process now has great influence among modern populations. For most employees, work has a generally unpleasant quality. If there is little Calvinist

impulsation to work among propertyless factory workers and file clerks there is also little Renaissance exuberance in the work of the insurance clerk, freight handler, or departmental store sales lady. . . . For the white collar masses . . . work seems to serve neither God nor whatever they may experience as divine themselves. In them, there is no taut will to work and few positive gratifications from their daily round.[21]

What rises to fill the vacuum left by the purposelessness of twentieth-century work is, according to Mills and Riesman, a personality-oriented society that now pursues leisure as compulsively as the nineteenth-century craftsmen once pursued their duties: a society that now consumes with the eagerness that the pre-industrial farmer once produced; a society that now measures personality (the ability to get along with others) as earnestly as the Puritan once measured character (the ability to sustain deeply internalized values). In the wake of the new industrialism, the work ethic—to say nothing of the strong, self-directed, tireless workers who upheld it—is left "in tatters . . . only common in rhetorical commonplaces in political invective."[22] Hardly the kind of stuff from which hardworking dramatic heroes are fashioned.

However, much of the drama of twentieth-century America reflects a serious concern with, if not an outright commitment to, the work ethic in its most traditional and, presumably, outdated forms. Although it is not by any means the sole concern of those modern dramas that embody work-related themes, traditional Puritan work values and the impact that modern, rationalized industrialization has had upon them take on far more significance in American drama than one might assign to "rhetorical commonplaces." Works by Miller, Williams, Shepard, Rice, Albee, and Hansberry, among others, speak directly to the meaning that modern Americans derive from their work. Mssrs. Rodgers, Mills, and others notwithstanding, there is an explicit belief among the major playwrights of this century that the modern American acquires a sense of himself, his family, his society, and his universe largely through his belief in the value of work and/or his job. If not altogether unaware of the conventional wisdom of twentieth-century social history, the American playwright is, at the very least, unpersuaded by it.

Several factors may acount for differences in the social vision of the twentieth-century American playwright, who sees individual attitudes toward work as vital to the consciousness of the twentieth-century American, and some leading social historians, who do not. To begin with, social scientists are not, by any means, unanimous in their view that modern American industry has so devalued labor that American workers no longer value work to any significant degree. Even Mills acknowledges that traditional work values, while having little economic influence on America, maintain a strong presence in the psychology and ideology of contemporary capitalism:

> As an economic fact, the old independent entrepreneur lives on a small island in a big new land; yet as an ideological figment and a political force, he has persisted as if he inhabited an entire continent. He has become the man through whom the ideology of utopia is still attractively presented to many of our contemporaries.[23]

Other historians go further, challenging outright the assertion that the work ethic is no longer a significant "economic fact" in American working life. Clark Kerr declares that the American worker is not, as Rodgers and Mills have suggested, moved by a "grudging acquiescence" but by an ideology and an ethic. It is Kerr's contention that the contemporary American worker has the same level of commitment to work as did his elders.[24] A somewhat qualified affirmation of this belief can be found in Chinoy's *Automobile Workers and the American Dream*, which argues that initiative, perseverance, and the desire for advancement may follow many factory workers throughout their working lives, particularly if they secure some form of wage or skill advancement at a relatively early age.[25] Dawley and Faler have gone so far as to propose that the work ethic has been intensified by modern industrialization, for it has forced the modern worker to "give up a casual work attitude and raucous mores for a new ethic of self-control, self-denial and self-improvement."[26] Thus, if those modern American dramatists who believe the work ethic to be important, if not vital, to the American psyche and the American character find themselves at odds with leading labor historians and social scientists, they do not, by any means, stand alone in open and unlettered defiance of the entire discipline.

More significantly, the dramatist, concerned as he often is with the individual's ability to resist the forces that try to mold him, is bound to run afoul of the social historian, who is often concerned with the extent to which individual character conforms to social character. One need look no further than David Riesman's classic study *The Lonely Crowd* to find a model for analyzing individual character in terms of social and cultural forces. But for a few followers of Brecht, American dramatists have tended to produce their best plays—even their best social plays—when they have examined Americans in heated battle against social forces.

This is not to suggest that modern American playwrights are indifferent to or unaware of the impact that twentieth-century American society has on the formation of the modern American character—especially where changes in modern work and work attitudes are concerned. Thirty years before Mills wrote of the impact that the widespread use of office machines would have upon the devaluation of white-collar clerical skills, Elmer Rice had given us *The Adding Machine* and Mr. Zero, whose humanity disappears as rapidly as his usefulness. Twenty years before David Riesman wrote of the pursuit of leisure that obsesses the successful American, Philip Barry wrote *Holiday*, whose hero, Johnny Case, declares that "one cannot work, earn, and *be* at the same time." And certainly

Willy Loman's frustration is tied to his intense desire to conform to a society whose conventions are far more subtle than he perceives them to be. But modern America also produced a number of depression playwrights, whose self-consciously radical politics constitute ringing endorsements of traditional, pre-industrial work values. Modern American dramatic literature also produces romantic heroes, such as Tom Wingfield in *The Glass Menagerie*, whose heroism is embodied in their unwillingness to surrender to the "character-shaping" social forces of the twentieth century.

American dramatists do not subscribe to a party line concerning the role of work in the shaping of American psyches and personalities any more than do social scientists. But there is among many of our finest playwrights a broad, and sometimes all-consuming, fascination with the subject. A study of this fascination and how it has manifested itself in the works of these artists can make few if any claims to contribute to our understanding of American social history since its domain is American social art—and solely dramatic art at that. But within that seemingly modest purview, there is important business to attend to. There is the need to bring into focus the modern American dramatist's collective statement of his time and his society—a generally neglected issue in the criticism of modern American dramatic literature. Moreover, there is the need to challenge the widely held notion that the intellectual and artistic quality of twentieth-century American dramatic literature as a whole is somehow lacking (and this I see as a major function of this book). And finally, there is the need to present to students of American society a complex and often overlooked portrait of that society—a portrait drawn by those people who make their living by creating pleasing, meaningful, lasting, and often profound visions of American life and American lives.

*   *   *

Introduction

A few brief definitions are necessary before we begin. The term *social drama* is being used here in a broad sense to mean a play (or plays) that, by design and intention, addresses itself to a specific problem in society or to the general nature of society; a social drama renders social commentary consciously. Granted, this definition makes for some strange bedfellows (Neil Simon and Imamu Baraka, for example) but it does so to allow for the broadest possible examination of the theme of work. I am aware that others, such as Arthur Miller and William Kozlenko, have offered very different definitions of the term *social drama*, and I have cited a few of these in relevant chapters. When I am referring to someone else's definition of the term, I will so indicate within the text.

Regarding the radical drama of the 1930s, I have accepted Morgan Himelstein's definition of *social realism* to define those plays that use naturalistic techniques to display on the stage Marxist fantasies of class conflict, racial solidarity, and so on. A very few other terms are used in this study and will be defined as they are introduced into the discussion.

I

WORK AND NINETEENTH-CENTURY AMERICAN DRAMA

The theme of work in modern American drama finds ample precedent in two major sources: One of these is the early naturalistic and realistic American drama of the late nineteenth and early twentieth century.[1] The other source, which we shall examine first, is the late nineteenth-century European playwrights such as Chekhov, Gorki, Shaw, and Hauptmann, who had raised the issue of the social, political, and moral dimensions of work in some of their plays.

Although his plays inspired very little stylistic imitation among dramatists prior to the Second World War, Chekhov, perhaps more than any other dramatist, introduced into his plays many ideas about work that eventually found their way into modern American plays. Nevertheless, in responding to social developments in their respective societies, both Chekhov and the modern American dramatists shared a vision of work as an abstraction: a vital but enigmatic part of the human character—a source of psychological and spiritual self-discovery over and above its economic significance. Chekhov was able to draw clear relationships between the vital changes occurring in Russia, which was moving at the turn of the century from a rural to an urban society and from an agrarian to an industrial society, and the psychological and social need for individual commitments to hard, meaningful work. As manifested in his major plays, his philosophy of work is broad, complex, and sufficiently self-contradictory to have anticipated nearly every major work theme in twentieth-century American drama: the strong endorsement of the Protestant work ethic in sentimental dramas, the protest against dehumanizing mechanization in expressionistic plays, the alternately radical and traditional politics in depression-era labor plays, and the existential consequences of work that are explored by post-World War II playwrights. But paradoxically, none of Chekhov's major plays takes place in a work setting, and throughout his plays one almost never sees on the stage anything resembling work.

One of the reasons so little work is actually done in a Chekhov play is that Chekhov is largely concerned with the effects of lack of work and productivity upon the individual. His particular fascination is with the peculiar state of living death that overcomes people of means who have nothing to do with their time and property. In *Ivanov*, for example, the title character realizes the dimensions of his paralysis when he falls in love with Sasha. The new vibrancy that Ivanov discovers within himself is expressed in terms of the life-giving value and importance of work: "It means to live again. Yes? To work again? Oh, my happiness, my youth, my freshness."[2] Moreover, when Sasha urges him to return to his wife so that he may reap some fulfillment in the few years left to him, she says,

> Go to your wife now and stay with her, and keep staying with her. But the main thing is don't forget your work.[3]

Sasha understands that productive work, more than love, will keep Ivanov from leading a sterile existence.

Chekhov expands the theme of lack of work and spiritual paralysis in *Uncle Vania*. In this play, Serebriakov's indolence saps the energy and vitality of everyone else who lives and works at his estate:

> Astrov [to Yeliena, Serebriakov's wife]. You just happened to come along with your husband and all of us who'd been working and running around and trying to create something, we had to drop everything and occupy ourselves wholly with you and your husband's gout. You

two infected all of us with your indolence. I was attacked by you and I have done nothing for a whole month, and in the meantime people have been ill and peasants have been using my . . . plantation as pasture for their cattle . . . So you see, wherever you and your husband go, you bring along destruction with you.[4]

Though Astrov may well be guilty of blaming others for his own weaknesses, his equation of "indolence" and "destruction" articulates a central comment that Chekhov is making about the social and psychological significance of work. More clearly stated here than in *Ivanov* is Chekhov's view that a lack of work, whether brought about by economic misfortune, spiritual weakness, or a combination of the two, is contagious in that it is the malaise of dying societies as well as of dying men. It spreads itself quickly and requires an enormous commitment of the will on the part of any person or any society that seeks to overcome it. In spite of Serebriakov's efforts to withdraw from society, he has spread his infection of indolence to everyone around him in the same manner that the aristocracy has infected all of Russia.

But Chekhov fully understands that a personal commitment to work is, if not a mixed blessing, certainly a highly compromised one. In *The Three Sisters*, Irena extols the virtue of all work when she senses that her life of inactivity is taking the meaning of life from her:

You know when I woke up this morning and after I'd got up and washed, I suddenly felt as if everything in the world had become clear to me, and I knew the way I ought to live. . . . Man must work by the sweat of his brow whatever his class, and that should make up the whole meaning and purpose of his life, and happiness and contentment. Oh how good it must be to be a workman, getting up with the sun and breaking stones by the roadside—or a shepherd or a schoolmaster teaching the children—or an engine driver on the railway. . . . Good heavens it is better to be a mere ox or a horse and work than the sort of young woman who wakes up at twelve and drinks her coffee in bed, and then takes two hours dressing . . . I long for work.[5]

But after she gets a job at the post office, the reality of real work strikes her, and she learns that work for most people in most circumstances is tedious and unfulfilling:

I must look for another job. This one doesn't suit me. It hasn't got what I always longed for and dreamed about. It's the sort of work you do without inspiration, without even thinking.[6]

The theme of disillusionment through work, or work as a source of unfulfilled wishes and unrealized dreams, anticipates the disillusionment and thwarted efforts of Willy Loman in Arthur Miller's *Death of a Salesman* and George in Edward Albee's *Who's Afraid of Virginia Woolf?* Moreover, the dullness and boredom of Irena's work prepares us for the German and American expressionists who will attack and expand this theme with a vengeance. But it must be noted that in *The Three Sisters* and elsewhere Chekhov finds a final reaffirmation of work as a soul-saving virtue that neither the expressionists nor the post-World War II American dramatists often embrace. At the death of her fiancé, Baron Toozenbach, Irena commits herself to a final affirmation of life—an affirmation made through a commitment to work:

We must go on living . . . and working. Yes, we must go on working. Tomorrow I'll go away and teach school. I'll give my life to people who need it. It's autumn now. Soon the snow will cover everything, but I'll go on working and working.[7]

Beyond the spiritual power of work to save a dying soul, Chekhov clearly sees work as having profound political consequences upon a society. It is in *The Cherry Orchard* that the revolutionary aspects of work are portrayed most forcefully. Paradoxically, Chekhov gives his most shrewd and accurate prediction of the twentieth-century society and its "problem-solving" mentality to the comical, even foolish Trofimov, the perennial student and knee-jerk radical. But Trofimov seems to articulate better than any other character in the play (or in any other Chekhov play) the role that work will play in the creation of the modern age:

> Everything that's unattainable now will some day become familiar and understandable: it is only that one must work and must help with all one's might. . . . With us in Russia so far only a few work. The great majority of the intelligentsia that I know are living for nothing, doing nothing and, as of yet have no capacity for work.[8]

Trofimov's speech is clearly self-serving. He is forever aggrandizing himself and justifying his prolonged adolescence in the name of waiting for the new age. But he accurately predicts the coming of a new social order that will be based on a capacity for work and a rejection of traditional Russian social values of noble privilege. So accurate was this prediction of events that later were to occur in Russia and so clearly does it explain the takeover of the estate by Lopahin that we can with some confidence attribute Trofimov's philosophical stance, if not his sillier characteristics, to Chekhov.

The revolutionary power of work as it is proclaimed by Trofimov is born out in practice by the efforts of Lopahin, the wealthy descendent of peasants. Lopahin is all business; his ambition, his drive, his faultless sense of timing in business matters, and his ability to act to insure the faultlessness of his timing enable him to stop the march of Russian history and stand it on its head:

> The cherry orchard is mine now. Mine. (Guffawing) My God, Lord, the cherry orchard is mine. Tell me I'm drunk out of my head. If only my father and grandfather could rise out of their graves and see this whole business, see how their Yermolay, beaten half-illiterate Yermolay, who used to run around barefoot in the winter, how that Yermolay has bought an estate that nothing in the world could beat. I bought the estate where grandfather and

father were slaves, where you wouldn't even let me in the kitchen . . . we are going to build villas and our grandsons and great grandsons will see a new life here.[9]

With the purchase of the Ranevskaya estate, Lopahin has symbolically purchased the new century and is prepared to develop it and shape it to his whim.

Other work-related themes that later appeared in American dramas are also found in Chekhov's plays and are worthy of some brief mention. In the thwarted, frustrated character of Serebriakov we find a clear relationship between a personal identity and success through work. ("I want to live, I love success, I like being a well-known figure, I like creating a stir."[10]) This theme became particularly important to post-World War II playwrights in America, such as Albee and Neil Simon, who explore the vulnerability of successful men to self-destruction through their work.

A similar example of such a man can be found in the character of the writer Trigorin in *The Seagull*. A self-proclaimed "writing machine," Trigorin confesses that the need to write is "devouring his own life." Trigorin's self-analysis not only anticipates the theme of work as a source of self-destruction that is to appear in twentieth-century American drama, but also hints at a protest of the mechanization of modern work, even work that is not machine oriented. Although by the 1890s much of America had been heavily industrialized, the mechanization of work and labor was not to become a major theme in American drama until the 1920s.

In a minor speech in *The Three Sisters*, Andrey Prozorov attacks class snobbishness regarding "respectable" and "disrespectable" types of work. When his family chides him for giving up his academic career for a small position with a local council in the town, Prozorov proclaims the dignity and importance of his work:

You seem to be annoyed with me for not making myself a professor. But I'm working in the council office . . . and

I feel my service there is just as fine and valuable as any academic work I might do . . . and if you want to know, I'm proud of it.[11]

While Prozorov is hardly an example of Mill's ceaseless, methodical Puritan, his speech echoes the secularized Puritanism of eighteenth-century America in its assertion that work per se, detached from any and all class stigmas, is decent and dignifying. This theme was to recur in various forms throughout the drama in America from 1920 to 1970.

Chekhov portrayed work not as a pathway to happiness but as a prerequisite for survival, survival that is difficult yet dignified. By establishing clear links between the importance of work to individual survival and the importance of work to the survival of an entire society, he opened the door for the modern American playwright to create plays of historical realism, character studies, and even propaganda based on work themes. Moreover, modern drama inherits from him the knowledge that in the modern age work, like love or religion, is one of those dimensions of life that is itself larger than life. Because of Chekhov the modern reader may hold the modern dramatist accountable for treating work as the complicated and explosive theme that it is.

The influence of Chekhov on work themes in modern American dramas is as subtle and indirect as many of his plays. While American dramatists to one degree or another may be influenced by Chekhov's intelligence and subtlety, many American authors have rejected his "mood plays" for action-oriented dramas in the mode of Hauptmann or Gorki. Of particular importance for our discussion here are Hauptmann's *The Weavers* and Gorki's *Enemies*, both of which anticipated labor plays and dramas of social realism that flourished in America in the 1930s and developed for America a solid body of plays based largely on work-related themes.

The Weavers depicts an onstage proletarian uprising

involving a revolt of hundreds of weavers employed by a cotton manufacturer named Dreissiger. Although the play lacks the specific ideological self-consciousness that was to be found in the American labor dramas, several characters, situations, and themes that were to become stock parts of those labor dramas occur in the Hauptmann play.

Generally considered to be a pioneering work of European naturalism, *The Weavers* presents in its settings a picture of worker poverty that is stark and riveting. As set forth in Hauptmann's stage directions, the sets "complement" the wretchedness of the lives of the weavers themselves:

> A small room in the cottage of Wilhelm Ansorage. The narrow room measures less than six feet from the dilapidated floor to the smoke blackened rafters. . . . A crippled old woman sits on a stool . . . the weak rosy light of the sun shines through two small openings in the left wall. These are partly pasted over and filled up with straw.[12]

The stark, naturalistic setting, particularly as it depicted the squalor of the working man's hovel, was to reappear in the works of many American labor playwrights including those of Clifford Odets and Elmer Rice.

The weavers' protestations about their life—a combination of articulate testimony of their own misery and a self-conscious plea for understanding of their rebellion—predate and anticipate the self-justifying statements of unionized workers in American labor dramas who excuse their revolutionary activities as they justify them:

> First weaver woman. I'm certainly not lazy but I just cannot go on this way much longer. I have had two miscarriages and my husband, he can't do more than half the work neither; . . . There's just so much a body can do. We sure do work as much as we can. . . . Everything will be all right if I can only get a bit of this weakness out of my bones. But ya got to have a little consideration.[13]

Like the union members of American labor dramas, the weaver woman avows loyalty to the socially acceptable value of hard work in order to prepare her audience for her imminent antisocial activity: a violent revolution against the Dreissigers.

A variety of characters in *The Weavers* was to become stock types in American labor plays. For example Pfeifer, the indifferent pay clerk, is the lowest member of management and is most anxious to dissociate himself from the people just below him:

> If it [the starvation wage paid the weavers] doesn't suit you, all you have to do is say the word. There are plenty of weavers, especially weavers like you. For full weight you'll get full pay.[14]

There is Dreissiger himself, a boss who thinks he is burdened with a life of grief but whose problems, when compared to those difficulties of squalor and poverty he has created for the workers in his employ, are laughably superficial:

> I couldn't put up with it [weaver unrest] any longer. This impudence simply goes beyond all bounds. It's shocking. I have guests and these radicals dare . . . they insult my wife when she shows herself. . . . I assure you if blameless people . . . such as me and my family . . . can be openly and continuously insulted . . . without proper punishment really.[15]

And, as we see in several depression-era radical plays, there is in *The Weavers* the character of the older worker who resists the sweeping tide of revolutionary fervor that is coming over the proletariat and, in resisting, is swept aside by the rushing tide of events:

> This is going too far. Downstairs they're already starting to break things up. It's crazy. There ain't no rhyme or reason to it. In the end that'll be a bad thing. Nobody with a clear head would go along. I'll be careful and won't take part in such goings on.[16]

It is ironic that Hauptmann himself took a similar position to that of the old weaver some forty years later when German playwrights were speaking out against Hitler. According to Block and Shedd, his refusal to join the protests may well be responsible for Hauptmann's relative lack of popularity among western readers, producers, and critics today.[17]

Hauptmann also gives to the radical drama in America the "moment of conversion," wherein a discontented but well-behaved worker, having reached the point at which conditions are intolerable, casts the die in favor of open revolution. Hauptmann skillfully exploits all of the dramatic tension and character development that such a moment invites and paves the way for similar conversion scenes in Odets's *Waiting for Lefty*, Ben Bengal's *Plant in the Sun*, Elmer Rice's *We, the People*, and other works:

> Ansorage. There must be a change, I tell ya, here and now. I won't stand for it no more. We won't stand for it no more, come what may.[18]

But more than anything else, what the labor drama of the 1930s owes to *The Weavers* is Hauptmann's use of onstage violence to bring the action of the play to its shocking, kinetic conclusion. Unlike Gorki's *Enemies*, a politically oriented labor play that uses the classical method of having news of murder and violence brought to the stage via messenger (see discussion below), *The Weavers* provides us with full onstage mob hysteria, panic, and even death. In the final act of the play a horde of marauding weavers storms the Dreissiger's house and heads for the outlying areas of the city, burning, shooting, and yelling along the way. The mob is heard gathering in the wings and then flows onto the stage. During this scene rocks and bullets fly through the window, and a terrified witness reports the details of the offstage violence that are too extravagant for staging (the burning of barns, for example). A final volley catches an elderly weaver sitting in his living room, and he dies onstage.

The noise and energy of *The Weavers* were to become a trademark of the radical social dramas of Langston Hughes, Clifford Odets, Albert Maltz, and others. Moreover, they were to give to that genre of plays a vitality and energy that even detractors of left-wing drama concede enhanced the artistic development and even the commercial appeal of the American drama of the 1920s and 1930s. To the extent that so many American dramatists were able to adapt Hauptmann's energetic staging to American situations and American characters, the "noisy" American drama (as Krutch has called it) seems to owe much of its noisiness, if not its "Americanness," to Hauptmann.

If the fire and rage of American radical labor dramas find a precedent in *The Weavers*, their self-conscious Marxism finds precedence in such plays as Gorki's *Enemies* (1906). Written shortly after Gorki's own involvement in the 1905 Bloody Sunday massacre in Russia (his apartment was a hiding place for worker leaders both in the massacre and in the general strike that followed shortly thereafter), the play is largely concerned with demonstrating the veracity of somewhat overly simplified Marxist credos. The play centers on a factory lockout in turn-of-the-century Russia, in which a middle-management official of the factory is killed by workers. Gorki sets out to convince the audience that the insensitivity of the factory bosses created the situation in which the official was killed, and thus Gorki seeks to place blame for the killing upon the capitalists.

The scenes of discontented workers and self-serving owners talking among themselves reveal many of the Marxist themes that were to become cornerstones of the left-wing theater of the depression years. Among them are the incompatibility of justice and expansive business practices:

> Mikhail [a partner in the factory to a pro-worker friend]. It's a question of good business practice not of justice. I tell you that your idea of justice is the ruination of good business.[19]

Gorki's capitalists also pose the thesis that the relationship of a worker to his boss is parallel to the relationship of a slave to his master: "Who are the masters of this world, you and I or the workers?"[20] And one of Gorki's older workers, Kon, laments with his comrades both the difficulty of common labor as well as the lack of dignity attendant to it, summing up in epigrammatic resignation, "There isn't any work, only orders."

But it is the speeches of Nadya, a strong worker sympathizer and the niece of a factory partner, that carry the heaviest messages of anticapitalist damnation and the historical necessity of violent proletariat revolution:

> Nadya [to workers being arrested]. Listen, you didn't kill him. It was them. They kill off everything with their greed and cowardice. [To the owners] It is you who are the criminals. . . . The killer's not the one who fires the bullet but the one who plants the bitterness.[21]

The overly self-conscious political theorizing in *The Enemies* renders it somewhat sluggish and far less compelling than Gorki's *Lower Depths*. And, indeed, heavy-handed Marxist polemics simply nagged much of the life out of many potentially exciting American labor plays whose authors could not bring themselves to suppress their dogma (Rice's *We, the People* is an example). In a sense American social drama inherited from Gorki a period of political puberty: a phase of overblown seriousness that is innocent and angry, and a little embarrassing in retrospect.

Although the strong left-wing bent of many modern American social dramas points to a strong ideological and artistic kinship between American social dramatists and Gorki or Hauptmann, American playwrights of this century were as likely to be influenced by Shaw's *Mrs. Warren's Profession* as by any nineteenth-century European play. Widely known at the turn of the century in Europe and America for its controversial views on prostitution, the play also engages its two protagonists in a lively debate about the nature of work and the degree of self-esteem one can hope to gain from a lifetime of work. The young, ambitious Vivie, although somewhat crass in her unabashed and uncompromising materialism ("I must have work and make more money than I spend"), embraces the work ethic in its traditional, pre-industrial form—right down to fervent belief in the ability of individuals to control their own environment:

> Everybody has some choice, mother. The poorest girl alive may not be able to choose between being Queen of England or Principal of Newham; but she can choose between ragpicking and flowerselling according to her taste. People are always blaming their circumstances for what they are. I don't believe in circumstances. The people who get on in this world are the people who get up and look for the circumstances they want and, if they can't find them, make them.[22]

However, Vivie's mother, Kitty Warren, in defending her life of well-paid prostitution to shocked and disapproving Vivie, rejects the work ethic, which is taken by Shaw to be the prevailing belief in society even as late as 1898:

> What did [my sisters] get for their respectability. I'll tell you. One of them worked in a whitelead factory twelve hours a day for nine shillings a week until she died of lead poisoning. She only expected to get her hands a little paralyzed but she died. The other was always held up to us as a model because she married a government laborer in the Deptford victualling yard and kept his room and three children neat and tidy on eighteen shillings a week—until he took to drink. That was worth being respectable for, wasn't it?[23]

Turn-of-the-century audiences may have been attracted to the play's modern sexual attitudes, but it is in the play's questioning and examining of traditional, pre-industrial work attitudes and values that it really leaves its mark. Certainly, it is this issue, and not the defenses of prostitution or the hypocrisy of sexual moralizers, that is examined over and over again by Rice, Williams, Miller, Albee, Simon, and many others.

While the evolution of playwrighting in late nineteenth-century Europe is generally attributed to the contributions of a handful of innovative men making startling breakthroughs, the development of modern American playwrighting was a more gradual process. This more gradual development was the result of the slow maturation of an entire theater, including the growing sophistication of producers, actors, and audiences, as well as playwrights. As Garff Wilson writes:

> American playwriting saw no sharp break with the past. The influence of realism, which already had been seen in the stage effects of many melodramas, had been exerted in small ways before it altered the basic conventions of dramaturgy.[24]

The gradual evolution of modern American playwriting appears to correspond with, if it does not actually dictate, the slow evolution of the theme of work. From plot embellishment in simplistic melodramas of the mid-nincteenth century, work developed into a serious thematic and social issue in some American dramatists' early attempts at realism during the 1890s and early 1900s. By that time, James Herne and Clyde Fitch had begun constructing plots of internal motivation rather than external accident and coincidence. They also began to tone down the dialog from the bombast of the earlier melodrama. More significantly, social issues such as class distinction and business ethics were being explored seriously in such dramas as Augustin Daly's *The City* (1909) and Edward Sheldon's *The Boss* (1911). But like the growth of modern American drama itself, the development of the theme of work was a long, slow process.

In the early temperance melodrama *Ten Nights in a Barroom* (1858), author William Pratt extolled the work ethic and its attendant virtues, which are undermined by the drunkenness of wayward men. Mr. Slade, after many years as a hardworking, well-respected miller, hopes to avoid a life of hard work by opening a tavern in town:

> I got tired of hard work and, determined to lead an easier life, I sold my mill, bought this house with my money, and I find it an easy life. . . . Every man desires to make as much money as possible with the least labor.[25]

But Slade's defiance of the work ethic is cast back on him when a series of crises befalls his customers, including the death of a young girl who attempts to rescue her father in a drunken brawl in Slade's tavern. The havoc that the tavern wreaks upon the formerly good people of the town is enough to turn Slade's wife and son against him. But Slade steadfastly refuses to heed the warnings and scoldings of his family: "When I was a miller, she grumbled because I worked too hard; now she grumbles because I don't work hard enough."[26] It is ironically appropriate that Slade is killed during a brawl by his own son, himself a swaggering drunk. The death of Slade returns the townsfolk to their senses as they reaffirm their allegiance to fidelity, sobriety, hard work, and moral conduct.

While the themes, techniques, and structure of *Ten Nights in a Barroom* bear no relationship to those of any serious modern drama, the image it portrays of the ideal working man (a good provider, a good family man, firmly committed to hard work for its own sake) resurfaced intact in many labor plays of the 1930s. And certainly it is this very image that was to be the target of playwrights who sought to modify the traditional, pre-industrial work ethic or challenge it outright, such as Rice in *The Adding Machine*, Miller in *All My Sons*, and even Burrows and Weinstock in *How to Succeed in Business without Really Trying*.

Some early melodramas also anticipated the advent of the realist and naturalist movements that eventually destroyed melodrama. For example, Augustin Daly's *Under the Gaslight* (1867) introduced to American dramas some of the urban settings that were to become corner-stones of twentieth-century American naturalistic literature.

The plot of *Under the Gaslight* is conventional melodramatic fare: on the eve of her wedding to a wealthy young man, a wealthy young girl discovers that she is really the daughter of two impoverished street thieves who have come to claim her as their own. Her efforts to hide from them take her to a series of earthy urban locales such as a pier, a small cramped basement of an apartment building, and even "the Tombs," New York City's first city jail. While these scenes have none of the stark, horrifying poverty to be found in Hauptmann's *The Weavers*, they did represent an important step forward in American playwrighting—the movement out of the parlors of the American aristocracy and into the homes and hangouts of the working class. By the 1920s, the less glamorous settings of city life were quite familiar to American playwrights and playgoers.

The development of work as a serious social theme in early American drama is gradual, but it is by no means imperceptible. Two early plays that boldly dealt with the problems of work in the modern era are worthy of discussion here because they not only represent important breaks with the melodramas of the nineteenth century; they also anticipate work themes that were to recur throughout the American drama of the twentieth century. The two plays are Clyde Fitch's *The City* (1907) and Edward Sheldon's *The Boss* (1911).

The City is the story of the Rands, a small-town family who, after enjoying several generations of success in their own small community, are persuaded by their ambitious, "modern" son George to move to New York City and try to conquer the financial jungle of Wall Street. Ultimately, the forces of the city's corrupting influences, greed, and the grand scheme of events overtake George, and after some initial success he is brought down by his own unintentional chicanery. The play is in some respects a business morality play. But it presents a compelling and paradoxical view of the modern city as a place where economics, business, and finances are all out of the control of individual men, thus presenting the man of ambition with enormous opportunities and tremendous risks.

Among the specific work themes that are explored in *The City* is the theme of assertion of manhood and independence through work in the modern world. An argument between the senior Rand and George over whether or not George should risk the family fortune in the city is clearly a symbolic confrontation between nineteenth-century rural work attitudes and twentieth-century urban work attitudes:

> Rand. My father turned me loose without a cent to make my own way. Your father will leave you the richest man in the town—with the best established name, with two banks safe as Gibralter.
> George. What you don't realize is that I am starving after a fight and a struggle—for even bigger stakes than you fought for.[27]

But at the end of the play, when George has been brought down by his own ignorance and the chicanery of his business rivals, he does not blame the city for his fall. Like Trofimov in *The Cherry Orchard*, he understands that there is a historical and social transition at work and that it is up to the individual to carve out his own opportunity in the face of that transition:

> Don't blame the city. She gives the man the opportunity. It is up to him what he makes of it. The small town gives it too easy. But the city! A man goes to the gates and knocks—New York, Chicago, Boston or San Francisco—no matter what city it is so long as it is big, selfish, and self-centered. And she comes to her gates and takes him in, and she stands here in the middle of her marketplace—where Wall St. and Herald Square and Fifth avenue and the Bowery and Harlem and 42nd st. all meet, and there she strips him naked of all his disguises and all his hypocrisies, and she paints his ambition on her fences and

lights up her sky scrapers with it—what he wants to be and what he thinks he is and then she says to him, make good if you can or to hell with you. And what is in him comes out to clothe his nakedness, and to the city he can't lie. I know because I tried.[28]

Like Trofimov, George knows that the new century will be built upon ambition and hard work. The new age is to him as it is to Trofimov, so bold, so exciting, and so romantic that it is thrilling even to be crushed by the power of the new force. But to those later playwrights who do not view work in modern, urbanized America as romantic (Miller, Odets, and Rice), the brutal choice articulated by Fitch remains the same: "make good or to hell with you." Fitch knows as well as Rice or Miller or Albee that accepting the challenge of work in twentieth-century America can destroy a man; what separates Fitch from these later playwrights is that this insight is not upsetting to him. Such a defeat is ennobling to Fitch, not degrading. Where the modern reader might expect the class-consciousness of Marx in Fitch's *The City*, he is given the forced grandeur of Lord Byron. But as we shall see in chapter three, Marx is waiting in the wings.

One of the earliest examples in American drama of left-wing sympathies toward problems of modern, urbanized work is Sheldon's *The Boss*. It is a drama involving labor problems, the rise of an oppressed and noble proletariat, an explicit theme of family-work conflict, a Hauptmann-like riot (complete with rocks coming through a window), and other elements that were to become familiar features of dramas of social realism in the next thirty years.

Michael Regan, an up-from-the-slums Irish dock worker, has used his power on the docks to outsmart the aristocratic James Griswold family. Maneuvering himself into a position that enables him to seize control of the Griswold warehouse interests, he agrees to let the Griswolds stay on as his underlings on the condition that he can marry Emily Griswold, James's daughter who does volunteer work in Regan's old neighborhood slum. Although Emily hates Regan, she agrees to marry him so that her family can maintain some of its wealth and stature in the community.

The drama thereafter concerns Regan's vicious treatment of the men who work for him and their union activities in response to his treatment. Although no scenes take place in the work place or in the slums, the spirit of the American union movement is demonstrated in the play when a union spokesman comes to Regan's house to present him with the union's demands. Regan hits the man in the face as Emily comes to his rescue, lecturing her husband and the audience on the strength, nobility, and pitiful wretchedness of the union men in city factories:

> Emily. He's stunned. It's a fine thing to send a man back to his dying wife this way.
> Regan. Dying. But I thought you said [she had] bronchitis.
> Emily. It isn't bronchitis, it's pneumonia and it was wrought from cold and hunger. The doctor says she won't last over the week. She made him promise not to tell her husband until the end.
> Regan. Why?
> Emily. Because she didn't want to stand between him and his striker's work. That's what you're fighting and you'll never beat that spirit in a thousand years.[29]

For all his proworker sympathies, Sheldon cannot bring himself to give proletarian characters their own voices, nor does he portray them as having control over their own political activity. The union itself is not founded by the men but by an aristocrat, Griswold's son, who is avenging his family's defeat to Regan. Also, the case for unionism is pleaded by such bluebloods as sympathetic liberal Emily Griswold or kindly Archbishop Sullivan. As the scene above indicates, the only scene that even has a union man come forward to speak his own case calls for the union man to be knocked unconscious, leaving Emily Griswold to speak for him.

Even the proletarian riot in the final scene is made middle class and, thus, respectable. When Regan hears the rabble gathering outside of his house, he goes to a window and immediately picks out by name the pillars of the community that have joined in support of the workers' riot:

> There's Archibald Moughton, the vice-president of the First National. . . . And the fellow climbing the fence—isn't that Grayson, senior member of Grayson and Grayson and company. . . . And look there. Strikers, gentlemen and toughs, scoopers and big businessmen.[30]

The vision of a senior partner of a corporation climbing the fence of another businessman's home at the head of a labor riot rather badly strains credulity, but it is clear that Sheldon had something more in mind here than photographic realism. In order to counterbalance his middle class audience's repugnance for worker strikes (if not for workers themselves), Sheldon had to soften the blow of this riot by sharing the workers' thoughts and actions with middle-class and upper-middle-class characters with whom the audience could identify and whose values they could accept. Later radical plays, as we shall see in chapter three, also were self-conscious about the social acceptability of the labor activities and the radical politics they advocated, and playwrights often had to soften their otherwise uncompromising dramas with an occasional foreswearing of allegiance to the American flag or to the virtue of hard work itself.

One of the curious aspects of the theme of work is that it is one of the few features of modern American drama that develops without the leadership of Eugene O'Neill. Although he is generally accredited with bringing American drama into the twentieth century, O'Neill had relatively little interest in exploiting work as a dramatic theme. His "merchant marine" plays (*Moon of the Caribbees* and *In the Zone*, for example) all but ignore the man-killing work of a seaman. His expressionistic play, *The Hairy Ape*, opens in a work setting but is ultimately concerned with a quest for identity that is entirely spiritual and is largely divorced from the issue of work. *Long Day's Journey into Night* and *Strange Interlude*, although concerned in part with materialism, do not take on the problem of work in any meaningful manner.[31]

The consequence of O'Neill's relative lack of interest in work is that this tradition of the Europeans (particularly Chekhov) was handed down to lesser men than themselves. It is, then, reasonable to argue that the slow, gradual evolution of the work theme is largely due to the fact that Americans such as Daly, Herne, Fitch, and Sheldon were not capable of producing great drama.

Lacking the attention and care of a single, great playwright, the theme of work developed in America through the work of a variety of playwrights with a rather wide range of artistic intentions, political ideologies, and playwrighting talent. As we shall see later, by the 1930s the theme of work had found its way into every imaginable genre of playwrighting. If Chekhov's plays inspired no single intellectual or artistic heir to his throne, they cut the path for imaginative, energetic explorations of the theme of work by many American playwrights going in many different directions. One of the first of these was Elmer Rice.

II

ELMER RICE

The reputation of Elmer Rice (1892–1967), as both a master of the dramatic art and a writer of important social drama, has been dwarfed by the reputations of some of his contemporaries: specifically, Eugene O'Neill, Thornton Wilder, and Clifford Odets. Alongside O'Neill's work, Rice's plays are unquestionably of secondary status. Rice, who was not given to modesty when speaking of his own work, joined all other serious critics in his assessment of O'Neill as the most important American dramatist of the age.[1] Furthermore, Rice's heralded experimentation in dramatic technique and dramatic form is arguably less successful than that of Wilder, who did not allow his technical innovations to draw attention from the overall impact of his plays, a common failing in Rice's work. However, Rice's secondary status as a social dramatist (more or less "tied for second" behind Odets with every other competent social dramatist of the 1920s and 1930s) is another matter.

Rice's social plays, and his dramatic presentations of the theme of work in particular, are collectively among the most varied, the most thoughtful, and the most innovative American social dramas of the century. In his forty-year career as a playwright, Rice incorporated an exhaustive number of social issues into his works, including pacifism (*The Iron Cross*, 1915), feminism (*The Seventh Commandment*, 1913), the court system (*Counselor-at-Law*, 1931), anti-Nazism (*Flight to the West*, 1941), Soviet-American relations (*Between Two Worlds*, 1934), child labor (*The House on Blind Alley*, 1916), suburban living

(*Close Harmony*, written with Dorothy Parker in 1924), and artistic expatriatism (*The Left Bank*, 1931). His classic *Street Scene* (1929) has become the model for the tapestry of ethnic urban "types" that characterizes later plays such as Kingley's *Dead End* (1935) and Blitzstein's *The Cradle Will Rock* (1936) as well as countless motion pictures and television programs. But his two plays dealing with work in contemporary America (*The Adding Machine*, 1923, and *We, the People*, 1933) represent Rice's most important contribution to the development of American social drama.

In his autobiography Rice describes a visit he made to the Chicago stockyards during a tour of his first play, *On Trial*:

> In the canning section a young man sat beside a vat through which sealed cans of beef stew moved on a belt. Open-eyed and open-mouthed he watched for air bubbles, snatching out the imperfectly sealed cans, a horrible picture of imbecility. I felt strongly about the stultifying effects of industrialism; the moronic boy for me personified the evils of the machine age. . . . I have always disliked mechnical devices and the system that produces them on psychological, moral, and aesthetic grounds.[2]

Rice claims, somewhat overdramatically, that this moment was an epiphany for him. He had come to see American industrialism and the American way of work not merely as an economic issue but as an assault on the entirety of human experience. Sanity, morality, and aesthetics were all potential victims of the machine age.

Rice's attitudes about American industrialization were to manifest themselves in different ways in his two major plays on the subject. In *The Adding Machine* he approaches work in terms of its humanistic conerns, that is, its impact upon the souls and psyches of working men. In *We, the People*, the most ambitious and far-reaching American play in the agitprop tradition, Rice explores the political dimensions of working life in America. As we shall see in the following discussion of the two plays, each play makes a seminal contribution to the development of the theme of work in American drama.

As is often the case with literature that is both excellent and popular, *The Adding Machine* enjoys two very different types of reputation among its academic and non-academic admirers. The play has continued to receive academic interest because it is, along with O'Neill's *The Hairy Ape* (1921), among the first American plays to embody the themes, dramatic techniques, and point of view of the German expressionist playwrights.[3] In response to questions and challenges by scholars, Rice has denied the direct influence of German writers while simultaneously admitting that certain similarities exist between the *The Adding Machine* and German expressionist works such as Georg Kaiser's *Gas* trilogy (performed in Germany during World War I) and *From Morn to Midnight* (which played in New York in 1922). Rice claims he was not aware of these similarities until after he had written *The Adding Machine*.[4]

In any case, the scholarly interest in *The Adding Machine* as an artifact of the expressionist movement in American drama has drawn attention away from the play's raison d'être: Rice's personal vision of the American world of work. It is, in fact, the compelling picture of the American office and the American office worker that has given this play its immense international popularity. In the fifty-nine years since it was written, it has been produced somewhere in the world almost every year. In the late 1950s and early 1960s, it enjoyed an astonishing surge of popularity—ninety-two productions between 1955 and 1965. Citing the play's central work theme, the author attributed the burst of popularity in the 1950s to the contemporary concerns over automation and the birth of the frighteningly surreal computer age.[5]

The Adding Machine concerns the fate of a modern everyman, Mr. Zero, who for twenty-five years has added columns of figures for the same company, sitting at the same desk in the same office without missing a day. But for all his years, Mr. Zero has learned nothing of himself or his work. Expecting to be rewarded for his loyalty and promoted for his efficiency on the twenty-fifth anniversary of his tenure with the company, he is instead informed by his boss (who, after twenty-five years, cannot remember Zero's name and can barely remember his face) that he will be replaced by a new adding machine. Mr. Zero murders his boss, presumably out of revenge and frustration. It is important to note that the murder occurs offstage between scenes. At no time does Rice allow Zero to exhibit passion, anger, or assertiveness. Thus the murder of the boss is less a development of character than it is a device for advancing the plot.

The remaining two-thirds of the drama take Zero through a series of grotesque, expressionistic scenes designed to demonstrate that Mr. Zero, and modern industrialized man, are hopelessly trapped "slave souls—both the raw material and the product of [their] age." [6] Zero is tried for the murder by a jury of his peers (Mr. One, Mrs. Two, and so on) where his defense of his actions and his justification of his existence are reduced to a pathetic recital of his work routine:

> One week's vacation with pay and another week without if you want it. Who the hell wants it? Layin' around the house listen' to the wife tellin' you where to get off. Nix. An' legal holidays. I nearly forgot 'em. New Year's, Washington's Birthday, Decoration Day, Fourth of July, Labor Day, Thanksgivin', Christmas. Good Friday if you want it. . . . An' when a holiday comes on Sunday, you get Monday off, so that's fair enough. But when Fourth of July comes on a Saturday, you're out of luck on account of Saturday bein' a half day anyhow, get me? Twenty-five years. I'll tell you something funny, Decoration Day and Fourth of July are always on the same day of the week. Twenty-five years. [7]

Zero is found guilty and is promptly executed for his crime.

After his execution Zero finds himself in the afterlife,

where his freedom from the constraints of life affords him the opportunity to find the love, warmth, and contentment he could only wish for during his lifetime. But his twenty-five years of adding figures has altered his soul forever, and he is incapable of taking any action that would restore his dignity or offer him the slightest bit of succor. When faced with the option to stay forever in the Elysian field in the company of a woman coworker he had always loved in life, he refuses. Even as an immortal being, Zero surrenders to the repression and self-denial he learned in his twenty-five years on the job:

> Zero. Say, you don't mean you want to stay here, do you, with a lot of rummies, loafers, and bums?
> Daisy. We don't have to bother with them. We can just sit here an' listen to the music. . . .
> Zero. I thought I heard it but I don't hear nothin' now. What's the quickest way out of this place?[8]

Fleeing from paradise, Zero finally finds himself in an office similar to the one in which he worked during his lifetime. He is sitting at an enormous adding machine, and the room is covered with reams of used adding-machine tape. It is here that Zero learns he is being prepared for his reincarnation. The "presiding officer," Lieutenant Charles, informs Zero that his soul (like the souls of all men) is recycled thousands of times until it is used up. Charles offers Zero another life at an adding machine along with the empty promise of an attractive blonde office mate. Zero, the eternal moron, enthusiastically accepts the offer, and the play ends as Zero runs joyously back to "his sunless groove"—another lifetime of paralysis, routine, and degradation.[9]

Rice's method of rendering his social commentary in *The Adding Machine* has an effective double edge to it. Accompanying Zero's perpetual state of self-delusion, misguided judgment, impotent protestation, and woefully inaccurate self-analysis are the analyses of articulate, incisive minor characters who balance Zero's grotesque stage presence with compelling insights into his life and his world. Most important among these characters is Mrs. Zero, whose astounding fifteen-hundred-word marathon nag constitutes the entire "dialogue" of the first scene. Although she is as frustrated by Zero's working life as Zero is himself, she is more powerful than he is and much more aware of what is happening to both of them. In contrast to Zero's belief that the boss is about to reward him for his loyalty and longtime service, Mrs. Zero reveals to us the awful truth:

> Well I've been waitin'—waitin' for you to get started see. It's been a good long wait too. Twenty-five years! An I ain't seen nothin' happen. Twenty-five years in the same job. Twenty-five years tomorrow. You're proud of it ain't you? Twenty-five years in the same job and never missed a day. That's somethin' to be proud of, ain't it. Sittin' for twenty-five years on the same chair adding up figgers. What about bein' store manager? You forgot about that didn't you. . . . Seven years since you got a raise. An' if you don't get one tomorrow, I'll bet a nickel you won't have the guts to go an' ask for one.[10]

Mrs. Zero's harangue is as unbearable as it is true. Rice invites us to conclude that Mr. Zero starts every working day listening to his wife's deadly accurate reminders of how worthless their existence is, and, of course, these reminders are every bit as oppressive as the working day itself.

But Mrs. Zero is as much a victim as she is a victimizer. While she has enough strength of character to assert herself in her expression of hatred and resentment against her life, she lacks the power and insight to direct her anger anywhere but against Mr. Zero, thus making both his life and her own worse than they already are. When she finishes her tirade at the end of scene one, we have heard nothing from her husband, and we have seen only his head peeking out from beneath the sheets. But we know already that neither character stands a chance of triumphing, progressing, or even surviving in the life that Mrs. Zero has so shrewishly, yet so precisely, outlined for us.

Complementing Mrs. Zero's bitter analysis on the state of Mr. Zero's existence in the world of work are the vicious appraisals of modern man rendered in the afterlife by Lieutenant Charles. As Charles sardonically describes for Zero a "super-hyper-adding machine" (that calculates the output of all miners in the world with only the "slightest pressure of the great toe of your foot"), he is repulsed by Zero's enthusiasm for such a great technological advancement. Disdainful of the accountant for not understanding that the development of such machines is the very source of modern man's undoing, Charles condemns Zero and all modern society with a vicious attack that speaks for the outraged and cynical author:

> You're a failure, Zero. A failure. A waste product. A slave contraption of iron and steel. The animal's instincts but not his strength and skill. The animal's appetites but not his unashamed indulgence of them. True, you move and eat and digest and excrete and reproduce. But any microorganism can do as much. Well time's up. Back you go to your sunless groove—the raw material of slums and wars—the ready prey of the first jingo or demagogue or political adventurer who takes the trouble to play upon your ignorance and credulity and provincialism. You poor, spineless, brainless boob—I'm sorry for you.[11]

Paradoxically, these antihuman speeches of Lieutenant Charles carry Rice's humanistic concerns about the state of work in America. The boredom and bitterness so prevalent in the speeches of Mrs. Zero and in the behavior of Mr. Zero not only cause poverty and frustration; they also lower the state of the species of man. Dehumanization by work is not merely a metaphor to describe tedium and job routine. As far as Rice is concerned, the routine of office work lowers man on the evolutionary scale, diminishing his capacity for survival, increasing his vulnerability to attack and destruction, and crippling his body-saving instincts as well as his soul-saving insights. The "virtue" of work for its own sake and the "sanctity" of self-denial seem to be killing us.

Zero's failure to comprehend Charles's message is the ultimate degradation that modern rationalized industry heaps upon modern workers. Zero begs for an escape from his purposeless life and is ultimately satisfied with the promise of a repetition of it. What is more, and what is worse, Zero has confused the re-entry into monotony with an escape from monotony. Mr. Zero cannot survive, not because he does not want to but because he does not know how to. It is this aspect of working life that so terrifies Rice and so effectively drives this play.

The imagination and force that Rice employs to drive home his message in the play are so effective that *The Adding Machine*, both in production and in reading, survives its structural looseness, its gross character inconsistency (for example, the ineffectual Zero committing so revolutionary an act as killing his boss for not giving him a raise), and its complete avoidance of subtlety. But more importantly, the drama is so incisive in its attack on the nature of work in modern society that it survives its equally difficult obstacles of total lack of objectivity and total lack of compassion. Rice expresses his protest against the devolution of man by creating a drama of unrelenting nihilism peopled by misanthropes who are only funny in the grotesque and only appreciable to the degree that Rice can depreciate them.

It is Rice's unique approach to the world of work that permits, and even encourages, his audience to endure some of the play's otherwise unendurable moments and to forgive some of its otherwise unforgivable failings. To begin with, the play's emphasis on humanistic and moral concerns shifts all focus away from the conventional economic issues that a reader in the 1920s might normally associate with a play about work and working life. Downplaying the employer-employee conflict, even minimizing the oppressive poverty of the Zero household, and wholly dismissing the tenets of the work ethic, Rice makes us concentrate on the universal question of the fragility and vulnerability of human dignity. Both reader and spectator come away from this play—which begins, develops, and concludes with problems of the workaday world—only secondarily concerned with workers' rights or capitalist oppression. Instead, he is fearful of the state of his own soul and worried about the nature of his being.

The idea that modern work creates havoc with the soul and with the social order was a new and important concept in American drama. *The Adding Machine* was the first American drama to portray modern mechanized work as an alien and undefeatable foe of the worker, even though historians believe that American workers had resigned themselves to this belief as early as the mid-nineteenth century. Whereas conventional protest dramas, melodramas, and even "cup-and-saucer" comedies portrayed the business world as the product of the follies or injustices of fallible, mortal, and even defeatable men, the economic system in *The Adding Machine* is born of the cosmos. It is "manned" by demons in the afterlife against whom no one can contend, much less win. To survive is to capitulate to their will; to capitulate is to lose one's soul. It is not until a confused, entrapped Willy Loman realizes in 1949 that "something is happening" to him that the world of work is again dramatized as an incomprehensible force that tests the universal dignity of a man. As we shall see in a later chapter, *The Adding Machine* both anticipates and influences works by such recent dramatists as Albee and Miller. By bridging the particulars of contemporary American working life with the universal concerns of man's identity and man's dignity, *The Adding Machine* in fact lays crucial artistic and philosophical groundwork for some of the most important social dramas of the post-World War II period.

A decade after *The Adding Machine* was produced, Rice achieved a measure of critical success with his play *We, the People*. A stormy, if minor controversy occurred in 1933 when Burns Mantle decided to include *We, the People* in his prestigious, annual volume of *Best Plays*. Mantle, whose influence in New York theater circles was considerable and whose selections were an important annual event, came under fire both for ignoring the dozens of more successful plays that opened that season and for even considering a play that closed in six weeks to reviews that could be described at best as mixed. But Mantle stood firm, arguing in his introduction to *Best Plays of 1932–1933* that the play was not only an important social drama but was, in fact, important to social drama. Mantle argued that by lending the suspect genre of realistic, social protest plays his intelligence, his prestige, and his skill, Rice had asked new questions about the artistic importance and "respectability" of the entire genre, and thus had raised the stature and importance of all social drama.[12] Mantle's assessment was entirely correct and universally ignored. Since the opening of Odets's *Waiting for Lefty* in 1935 (the most famous radical drama of the 1930s), *We, the People* has virtually disappeared from critical and scholarly discussions of American drama, save only passing mention in a few full-length studies on Rice and the author's deathbed defense of the play in his 1963 autobiography.

Written in 1932 and produced in 1933, *We, the People* was in many respects a typical labor drama, a genre of social protest that was popular in the 1930s and was born out of the political issues of unemployment and worker exploitation that were important to left-wing thinkers and writers of that time. Strongly influenced by this rather primitive radical art form, Rice stocked *We, the People* with characters, speeches, and devices common to the plays of the militant labor theater groups: humble working people spouting Marxist rhetoric, public-be-damned capitalists diabolically protecting their own interests, and the obligatory final "meeting" scene in which the characters address a gathering of citizens (played by the rarely unwitting and never unwilling audience) and urge them to action.[13] But within the confines of this seemingly limited genre, Rice managed to endow his play with literary and intellectual innovations that carved out important territory not only for Odets (whose debt to this play is considerable) but also for many other left-wing labor playwrights.

To begin with, the plot of *We, the People* is very complex—a rarity in labor plays, which often featured insultingly simplistic story lines. Helen Davis is a young teacher who lives with her family. At the opening of the play, her family is prospering through ambition and hard work. Her father, a factory foreman, appears to have a secure job, even though the factory is experiencing marginal layoffs. Helen, although her paychecks are a few months behind because of a financially strapped city school system, is making do and is enjoying her professional status as well as the security of her job as a schoolteacher. Helen's younger brother Allen is a brilliant, ambitious college student. Because of jobs the family members hold at the beginning of the play, each seems to be endowed with the strength of character to weather hard times.

In contrast to the Davis family is the family of Bert Collins, Helen's fiancé. A struggling young banker, he has virtually no future with his bank because no opportunity for advancement is open to him. Moreover, his family is falling apart. Older brother Larry, left impotent and partially paralyzed from gassing in World War I, cannot work, is going insane with bitterness and despair, and is ruining the lives of his wife and son in the process. The contrast between the Davises and Collinses is underscored shortly after the play is underway: at the same time that Larry is committed to an institution after beating his wife and causing his son to run away from home, Helen Davis receives several months' back pay from the schoolboard.

But the initial contrast between the Davis and Collins families is quickly undercut, for the hard, fast collapse of the pathetic Collins family signals the steady erosion of the strong foundation of job security upon which the middle-class aspirations of the Davis family have been built. Over a period of twelve scenes, Mr. Davis is forced to take a 10 percent pay cut, which he cannot afford yet cannot combat ("There's nothing to do but take it and keep quiet"). To make up the difference, Mr. Davis takes in a boarder, an unpleasant man who quickly turns the happy, contented household into a place of tension and anxiety. Later, Helen Davis and Mr. Davis both lose their jobs, forcing Allen to drop out of school and to get a job that does not pay enough to feed the family or heat the house for the winter. Allen is later jailed briefly for stealing coal, but his convict status soon makes him a suspect for a murder he did not commit. Ultimately he is convicted for murder since, as an ex-convict, he is an unreliable witness in his own defense. By the end of the play, the hardworking, prospering Davis family is in shambles.

Interspersed among the scenes depicting the gradual demise of the Davis family, Rice develops a subplot involving an antiworker conspiracy. A group of local government, business, press, and academic leaders attempt to get one of their friends elected to the Senate so that he can bestow political favors on the others. While such a story is a common feature in strike dramas, Rice introduced another interesting feature. He was particularly concerned about the compromising of a university in such a practice; thus he examined in the play conflicts experienced by professors who choose to speak out against university participation in various business practices. This was to become a recurring theme in later labor plays written by middle-class, university-educated writers for university-educated audiences, such as George Brewer's *Peace on Earth* and Paul Green's *Enchanted Maze*. Rice extends this subplot to the point that it even touches on themes of anti-Semitism: A Jewish professor is expelled for criticizing the university's association with a ruthless businessman; a WASP professor from a proper family is only given a mild reprimand.

In the final scene, all the protesting, disenfranchised,

and oppressed characters gather at a town meeting, at which time Rice tries to tie together the gross expanse of social themes he has introduced into the drama. It is Rice's hope that the group appearance of Helen Davis, the Jewish professor, the WASP professor, and a strike organizer from Mr. Davis's plant will bring about the thematic and political unity he is seeking. But it is here that the play actually fails as agitprop drama. Rice's stilted dialog can only convert the already converted. Moreover, the number of issues (which by now include feminism, pacifism, and race relationships in addition to strikes, free speech, and the futility of middle-class ambition) is so unwieldy that acceptance of Rice's viewpoint would not only require more effective persuasion from the author but also several years of acculturation to 1930s New York liberalism on the reader's part.

But even in its failure to persuade, *We, the People* expanded the form and content of the labor drama on several fronts. To begin with, it was the first major labor drama to weave together a series of related left-wing issues in a single play instead of limiting its focus to the labor-management, class-consciousness issues of the conventional labor play. Later plays seized upon this expansion of issues in an effort to unify disparate segments of society in a left-wing struggle and to convince the audience that evil capitalist practices are pervasive in society. Playwrights such as Odets, in *Waiting for Lefty*, and Blitzstein, in *The Cradle Will Rock*, managed this technique more successfully than Rice did in *We, the People*.

But the most remarkable achievement in *We, the People* is the deft handling of the contrasts between the Davis and Collins families. Deliberately establishing a deceptive contrast between the two families at the opening of the play, Rice brilliantly undercuts the audience's expectations by chipping away gradually at the Davises' Puritan values of hard work, careful planning, frugality, and faith in education. By the end of the play the audience realizes that the lower-class Collinses are not the opposite of the middle-class Davises; they are in fact the Davises in an advanced state of social and economic decay. Because this ironic development occurs gradually, it is probably more clearly realized in the reading of the playscript than in the viewing of a production (it went virtually unnoticed in the reviews of the production but in the text it is unmistakable).

The gradual elimination of the contrast between the Davis and Collins families not only makes for an effectively written play but also advances Rice's thesis that the only thing separating the values and attitudes of the middle class from those of the lower class is job security. In *We, the People* middle-class values of hard work, education, and moderation in politics and social behavior are not an "ethic" but rather a luxury of the gainfully employed. When unemployment hits the Davis home, Allen, the future doctor, abandons his studies and begins to steal; Helen, who teaches blind patriotism to her students in the play's opening scene, calls a radical protest meeting after she is fired; and the long-suffering Mr. Davis joins the strike in his plant.

The Davis-Collins juxtaposition not only endows the play with a highly sophisticated social thesis but also gives an entirely credible depiction of the futilty of middle-class ambitions during hard times. The episodic structure of the play (twenty scenes, no acts) shows the Davises falling gradually, fending off one crisis after another, making some marginal progress on occasion while never really knowing if they are in serious danger or not. The assault on their ideals and their emotions as well as on their financial resources is gradual but relentless, catching the unsuspecting reader as well as the unsuspecting family in the false faith in the ability of upright, hardworking folk to weather any storm.

Although Rice's politics are similar to those of other left-wing dramatists of the 1930s, his portrayal of the road to poverty is far more ambitious and intelligent than the conventional labor drama portrayal of hard times during the depression. Normally, labor dramas "open on" families after disaster has struck and the principals are already near destruction. The economic and psychological processes by which a family discovers that it lacks the power to sustain itself is sidestepped entirely. In *We, the People*, however, the conflict between false hope and nagging uncertainty is given sufficient time and attention to provide insight and warning for the hardworking, security-minded middle-class job holder or playreader. The conflict develops slowly enough to demonstrate the economic links between the middle class and the lower class that Rice sees as so important. Moreover, the play represents one of the first attempts to endow characters in labor plays with complex, credible motivations and responses.

We, the People also achieved a minor but noteworthy breakthrough in its handling of race relations in 1930s drama. In one scene, Larry Collins rails at Steven, a black deliveryman who by his mere presence reminds Larry of his own poverty and bitterness. Larry's bitterness, which he turns on anything and everything, has made him viciously racist. With no provocation, Larry screams at Steven, "I may be low but I don't have to take nothing from no nigger." In a later scene Larry chases the man out of the house. These two scenes indicate Rice's understanding that the tensions of urban poverty and unemployment that whites and blacks share are more likely to aggravate racial animosities than ease them. Such a view is in stark contrast to most labor plays dealing with racial themes (Maltz's *Stevedore*, Lawson's *Marching Song*, Hughes's *Scottsboro Ltd.*), which hold that blacks and whites will unite in a brotherhood of workers to defeat oppressive bosses; *We, the People* leaves the hostility between Larry Collins and Steven with little hope of resolution. It is Rice's perception that has proved true during the past fifty years of race relations, not the left-wing fantasy.

As a result of its complex social doctrines and its sophisticated presentation of those doctrines the play holds a special place in the history of social drama in New York. It was responsible for a debate over whether dramas about social problems, heretofore confined to radical theater, had any place in the mainstream of New York's legitimate theater.[14] Among the critics arguing for the "legitimacy" of social drama was Richard Dana Skinner:

> The heaping up of all possible misfortunes on one family is a direct result of [Rice's] effort to view a national scene through a limited field. . . . In the last two years, as seldom before in our history, calamities have come in droves over single families. Mr. Rice has the objective facts to support the incidents of the play, enough even to justify the accumulation of disasters over a single home.[15]

Yet Joseph Wood Krutch had some reservations:

> We expect of a drama that it shall tell us something we do not know, or, if it deals wholly with the familiar, that it shall arouse and then discharge our emotions in some effective way. If it does none of these things, we may still approve as we approve *We, the People*, but we shall remain nevertheless unsatisfied.[16]

Debates over the value of social drama that dealt with "the familiar" were to continue in drama circles throughout the 1930s.

While the advances that Rice made in the development of the theme of work in American drama are most clearly demonstrable in the humanistic themes of *The Adding Machine* and the expansion of the labor drama genre through *We, the People*, he made other contributions to the development of this theme in other plays. *The House on Blind Alley*, an early work that is a farcical parody of Mother Goose that turns into a grotesque protest against child labor practices, was a failure by every standard. The play was too encumbered by its parodying technique to have much impact as social drama and too tiresome in its weak attempt to stage Lewis Carroll-like satire to inspire imitation. It is only noteworthy for its willingness to approach an issue that rarely surfaced in any form of radical literature of the 1920s and 1930s.

Of far greater interest and importance is a speech delivered by attorney-hero George Simon in the otherwise unimportant Rice play *Counselor-at-Law*. Depressed because he is facing a possible disbarment, George suddenly lashes out at the entire work ethic and the success he has achieved in his profession:

> Let them disbar me. What the hell do I care. I'll go on a boat somewhere and spend the rest of my life enjoying myself. Why shouldn't I? Ive been working like a horse ever since I'm eight years old. Why shouldn't I quit and see the world and have a good time? Why this thing may turn out to be a godsend for me: a chance to get out of the harness and live a life of leisure.[17]

The contemporary sound of George's plaint makes the speech noteworthy. *Counselor-at-Law* was written in 1931 when Americans were grateful to have work of any kind—to say nothing of a law practice—and aspiring middle-class families struggled to get their children into the professions. Although questioning of the work ethic from a position of relative affluence was to become a familiar theme in the 1950s and 1960s, Simon's speech stands as one of the earliest foreshadowings of the theme of dissatisfaction with hard-earned, middle-class success and prosperity.

It would be difficult to argue that Rice should or should not be "ranked" with Odets as the premier social dramatist of the 1930s. The two writers offer very different kinds of talents and have made very different kinds of contributions to the social drama of this century. Rice never matches the dramatic intensity of the protestations and self-assertions that stir in the souls of Ralph Berger in *Awake and Sing* or Ernst Tausig in *Til the Day I Die*. Rice's dialog at its best, as it is in *Street Scene,* is never truly passionate or visceral. At its worst, as it is in the climactic scene in *We, the People,* it is unforgivably rigid.[18]

Yet no social dramatist of the 1920s or 1930s can rival his intelligence or his vision. While not the equal of Ibsen or Chekhov, he is a worthy heir to that dramatic tradition that examines the interrelationships of historical circumstance and universal humanity. Moreover, he is among the most original and imaginative dramatists the country has ever produced, experimenting boldly with the dramatic technique (*On Trial, Subway, Street Scene*) as well as the thematic content of his plays. But since the left-wing drama of the 1920s and 1930s will most likely be remembered for its radical fire rather than its dispassionate intellect, Elmer Rice will probably endure as an anonymous and often unseen influence rather than a towering name.

III

TOIL AND TROUBLE
IN THE 1920S AND 1930S

Despite the tendency of critics and scholars to refer to the socially significant plays of the late 1920s and 1930s as a specific "movement," it is impossible to examine the dramatic literature of the period and say with any confidence that American social drama begins or ends at one point or another.[1] While the radical plays of the depression era constituted a discernible body of works with themes (and even certain dramatic techniques) that were particular to the decade and unprecedented before 1929, several writers of comedy and melodramas had concerned themselves with modern social themes as early as the close of World War I. Even if the impact of many of these plays as important social literature was blunted by oversimplification and sentimentalism (demanded by both the tastes of their audiences and the genres themselves), an early awakening of popular playwrights to the serious problems of unemployment, hunger, immigration, farm collapses, the takeover of the economy by Eastern industry, and even unionism predates the radical theater of the 1930s by at least a full decade. Moreover, some adventurous playwrights, most notably Eugene O'Neill and, as we have seen, Elmer Rice, had begun writing in the mode of German expressionism in the early 1920s and thus gave American drama an early if short-lived introduction to that form of social drama.

The early growth of a socially conscious American drama should be viewed, then, not as a single-purposed art of a single-minded radical movement, but as a chaotically democratic hodgepodge receiving contributions from the arch-conservative and the committed radical, the bold experimenter and the commercial hack, the wiscracking comedian and the brooding tragedian. As we shall see in this chapter, it is the result of the efforts of a number of playwrights with a wide variety of interests to stimulate and exploit man's normal interest in and knowledge of the society that he has created for himself. Thriving in its earliest stages on issues more than ideologies, social themes in American drama were nourished largely on such issues as the changing mores in sex and marriage, crime, and, central to our discussion, work. In an effort to account for the variety of artistic and philosophical approaches to work themes that we encounter in the drama of the 1920s and 1930s, I have organized the discussion of this period into somewhat flexible but easily discernible categories: conventional entertainment dramas and comedies, radical labor drama, and experimental plays.

The presence of work issues in entertainment dramas during the first thirty years of the century was itself a natural outgrowth of the melodramas of the late nineteenth century, which often featured dire consequences to families who could not reap a profitable harvest or appease a ruthless patriarch. A clear account of the continuity between the nineteenth-century melodrama and the development of the modern social drama appears in Lillian Sabine's *The Rise of Silas Lapham,* a 1919 adaptation of William Dean Howells's 1876 novel.

The plot of the play is more sentimental than that of the novel. Lapham, a self-made tycoon who has earned his fortune by his invention and manufacturing of a high-quality mineral paint, is faced with destitution and ruin when a rival paint company discovers natural gas on its property, thus enabling it to manufacture and sell a comparable paint at half the price. While despairing over what the financial and psychological consequences of destitution might mean to him and his daughters (one of whom is about to marry into a "proper," old-money Boston family), Lapham is presented to an Englishman who wants to buy his company at a handsome price. Fully aware that the Englishman knows nothing of his company's imminent ruin, Lapham anguishes over whether or not to "do the right thing" and inform the Englishman of the company's vulnerability or to take the money and save his considerable wealth and his daughter's opportunity for social advancement. Lapham decides to reveal his company's status to the Englishman and is ultimately rewarded spiritually and financially for his ethical behavior.

The play clearly owes much to nineteenth-century mores. Lapham is a wholly virtuous man who is tempted to fall from that virtue. His decision to act ethically in business reaffirms his goodness, which is buttressed further by the rewards he reaps from that deed. Nineteenth-century social themes are here too: the virtue of the self-made man and the class prejudice he suffers at the hand of aristocratic snobs who do not work for a living.

But for all the nineteenth-century concern with unblemished virtue and for all her naiveté about the kinds of business decisions a self-made tycoon would be likely to make in the face of financial disaster, Sabine has endowed this play with an important and profoundly modern theme—Lapham's existential self-identification with his paint (that is, his work). We learn in the opening scene that Lapham, at the start of his career, could not take on a partner even when he needed one because his sense of himself was too closely tied to the paint: "The paint was like my own blood. . . . I couldn't bear the idea."[2] So eager is Sabine to wed Lapham's identity to his product that she even allows the paint to supersede the issue of class when the old-money Bostonians snub him. ("I confess an aversion to descendants gilded with mineral paint."[3]) But the most important and the most modern aspect of Sabine's "emersing" of Lapham's identity into the product is that by doing so she links Lapham's family values and his work values, thus creating a tension between work and family that was to recur throughout the labor dramas of the 1930s as well as in plays of Williams, Miller, Albee, and others.

Throughout the drama, Lapham's primary concern is the effect of poverty and ruin upon his family: to be honest at work is to destroy the family and to protect the family is to be unethical at work. Yet Lapham's wife, Persis (for whom the paint is named and who symbolically unifies the work and family conflicts), convinces him that he cannot possibly help his family, himself, or his work by being dishonest even for the most noble reasons:

> Si, you named the paint after me because you said it was the best brand made—that this paint would keep faith with every man that ever bought a pound of it. You put my name on it . . . kind of made me a partner in it. Well we're partners in that girl in there too. What are you going to do? Try to make happiness for her by something she'll be ashamed of if she ever knows it. . . . If you can look at this can of paint, this Persis brand, and find it in your heart to do anything that ain't fine as the Persis paint, then you ain't the man I married.[4]

In a sentimental play such as this one, the virtues ascribed to the virtuous product are easily transferable to the virtuous family and vice versa. But in later realistic plays the oportunity for dramatic tension between home values and work values is exploited much more fully. In O'Neill's *More Stately Mansions*, the hero is driven to madness by his inability to distinguish between family conduct and business conduct.[5] In Miller's *All My Sons*, a family is destroyed by the father's failure to apply to his business the ethics he espouses in his home. It seems to be the fate of businessmen in modern American dramas to be forever grappling unsuccessfully with conflict of work and family values, unable to reach the premodern bliss of Silas Lapham's work-family unity or the Shavian iconoclasm of Andrew Undershaft's joyous work-family paradoxes.

In the 1920s and 1930s, some melodramas and other entertainment plays developed even more profound depictions of working life in modern America than Lapham's while maintaining their primary function as entertainment. Sophie Treadwell's *Machinal* (1928), ostensibly a melodramatic character study of "any young woman," borrows heavily in its opening scene from expressionist theater (and particularly from scene II in *The Adding Machine*) to dramatize the numbing noise and routine of office work—a routine that in both its militaristic order and its unrelenting dullness contrasts with the heroine's volatile inner thoughts:

> Stenographer. You're late!
> Filing Clerk. You're late!
> Adding Clerk. You're late!
> Stenographer. And yesterday!
> Filing Clerk. The day before!
> Adding Clerk. And the day before.
> Stenographer. You'll lose your job . . . Why are you late?
> Young woman. Why?
> Stenographer. Exuse!
> Adding Clerk. Excuse!
> Filing Clerk. Excuse![6]

Elliot Field's *Tenant Farmers* (1939) would be a typical mortgage melodrama if Field had not introduced characters who sit on the hero's front porch spouting folksy Marxist dogma while the insurance company closes in:

> Big machines that grind out profits. Machines know nothing but profits. Nothing about the toil and sweat and blood and tears of the men and women who slave to make those profits. . . .
> [If I ran the insurance company] I tell you what I'd do. I'd organize the company primarily on the basis of service, not profit. . . . I'd make my clients partners somehow. Some sort of co-operative perhaps.[7]

The anti-industrial, even pre-industrial, Marxism in this play (and in many of the radical social dramas of the 1930s that will be discussed later) reveals a conservatism that historian Warren Susman argues is a central but generally unrecognized reactionary strain undergirding the culture and politics of America in the late 1920s and 1930s.[8] Although it is conventionally considered to be a period when intellectuals in general and literary artists in particular embraced Marxism so forcefully as to give that period an indelible stamp of radicalism, Susman argues that the thirties revealed a desire on the part of Americans to escape from the growing bureacratization and mechanization of modern society and return to the small-town community of the pre-industrial age. Alienated from machines and growing cities, Americans turned to the myth- and symbol-making powers of photojournalism, films, and radio to create for them ideas and images to which they could become committed. Susman also points out that the 1930s saw a proliferation of conservative, self-help literature (Carnegie's *How to Win Friends and Influence People*, Pitkin's *Life Begins at Forty*) that extolled the virtues of self-reliance, advanced the belief that failure is caused by individuals and not by social environment, promoted the idea that work is basic to a meaningful life, and asserted that man has the power to control his environment and his destiny.[9] Stopping just short of calling the New Left of the 1930s a "surrogate religion," Susman suggests that the significance of the radicalism of this period may lie less in its ideological principles than its reactionary need to identify with traditional, manageable, familiar, meaningful ideas and symbols:

> Thus it was characteristic in the 1930s for the idea of commitment itself to merge with some ideas of culture and produce, at least for a time, participation in some group, community, or movement.[10]

To the extent that this pre-industrial conservatism is evident in 1930s drama, one can find no stronger piece of evidence than Sophie Treadwell's *Hope for a Harvest* (1938), which was published and produced by the Theater Guild. Intended to extol the virtues of hard work and self-discipline to a modern, spoiled society, the play becomes, in spite of itself, a racist rallying cry to WASPs who have been demoralized by the intrusion and success of hard-working immigrants. Treadwell assumes an orthodox liberal position when she has Elliott Martin, the hero of the play, recognize the narrow-mindedness of such racist slurs as "Dago" and "Jap," but she turns around and urges her white audience to conquer the immigrants by out-working them, outwitting them, and out-bargaining them in order to gain back the spirit of hard work as well as the white supremacist position of the founding fathers.[11]

If writers of conventional entertainment dramas in the 1920s and 1930s seemed to render commentary on the nature of work in a manner that was incidental to the entertainment value of their plays, writers of comedies were able to put the American work place and other work-related themes at the heart of their dramas. Concerned less with the themes attached to farm and rural settings that were often found in melodramas, writers of farce were by and large dyed-in-the-asphalt Easterners writing for the burgeoning class of white-collar workers that grew during the bureaucratization of modern industry in the early part of the twentieth century. From this group of playwrights came a "subgenre" of work comedy that I will call the *office farce*, a play characterized by a battle of wits between a free spirit who would rather be happy than wealthy and a straw-man business establishment that would prefer the hero to be wealthy and miserable.

Typical of the genre is one of its earliest examples, Mark Reed's *Let's Get Rich* (1920). Playing for a society ball, a starving, live-by-his-wits musician named Slocum Pope falls for Phoebe Curtis, the daughter of wealthy industrialist J. Warren Curtis. Curtis, displeased with Slocum's meagre fourteen-hundred-dollar-per-year income, gives him an ultimatum: he must become a wealthy man or he may not marry Phoebe. The ultimatum presents a difficulty for Slocum who, in the play's only serious scene, defies the stifling monotony of office work and the moralists who insist that he join the beleagured, joyless white-collar class:

> Phoebe. Haven't you any ambition?
> Slocum. I expect to be the only poor man left in five or ten years. Then think how conspicuous and famous I'll be.
> Phoebe. They'll probably put you in a cage so everybody can see you.
> Slocum. On exhibition. The lowest type to which an American can sink. A poor man. No, seriously Phoebe, I think I'm happier with my music, my job, and my friends.[12]

But Slocum accepts Curtis's challenge to become wealthy which, by virtue of his philosophy of life, is also a challenge to become wealthy without sacrificing his music, his friends, his spontaneity, or his joie de vivre. Slocum proceeds on his quest for wealth by executing some neat (if implausible) deceptions on his stodgy adversary. In addition to being a musician, Slocum designs buildings for a hobby, a hobby he uses to defeat Curtis. While it is perhaps unlikely that anyone untrained in architecture or uninterested in owning a home would have architecture as his hobby, it is essential to the office farce that the hero not participate in anything that remotely resembles routinized, ordered behavior. Slocum designs buildings for fun, a pastime that is not directed toward any of the more tangible ideals that early twentieth-century managers tried to impose upon their rural and immigrant employees— that is, steady daily work, job training, concern for long-range financial security, and so on.

Slocum persuades a wealthy developer to give him a one-million-dollar contract on the strength of his imminent marriage into the prosperous Curtis family and then immediately thereafter persuades Curtis to allow him to marry Phoebe on the strength of the imminent million-dollar contract. When Curtis and the industrialist client discover the ruse (which they do at a contract signing that occurs in Slocum's bogus office, staffed by "draftsmen" who are really members of the orchestra he plays in), they are too late to stop it. The press knows of the contract and the marriage, and the industrialists must either go through with both or face the embarrassment of being exposed as dupes. The play ends leaving the hero with the girl, the contract, the complete disdain of the hardworking, forever disapproving businessmen, and the fulfilled promise of wealth without work.

The office farce is an immensely appealing but deadly spoof of the work ethic in that it portrays the delicious fantasy of all office stiffs—a means of beating the system. This fantasy of reaping the rewards of work without work and living with the woman in Paradise is as bold a fantasy as beating "the rap" that God gave man in the Garden of Eden. With the same insight (but certainly not the same method) as the expressionist drama, the office farce makes its points by exploiting the routine and the lack of spontaneity. The life's blood that has been drained from the Mr. Zeroes has been restored in the Slocum Popes, who are not only out to get rich quickly but also to get rich joyously. In that they live by their wits and not their wages, they are wholly independent and thus embody an ideal of their audience, even if they embody it in a comic form.

The office farce might be considered significant social commentary by those who see the cardboard entrepreneur-manager-villain as the descendent of Mills's "ceaseless, methodical" pre-industrial Puritan, who consciously imposes the stultifying routines of office work upon the hapless office worker. And, indeed, Rich's caricature of J. William Curtis is not far removed from the Machiavellian picture we get of Frederick Taylor and the early followers of his scientific management principles in Braverman's *Labor and Monopoly Capitol*. On the other hand, the office farce loses some of its critical punch if one accepts the view expressed by Mills in *White Collar*. Mills states that by the 1950s the bureaucratization of work was so thorough that its routines and regimens were for the most part well beyond the control of the managerial classes, who were themselves victims rather than perpetrators of the system.

The office farce recurs throughout American comedy and musical comedy, from Kaufman and Hart's *Beggar on Horseback* in the 1930s up to the 1960s musicals *How to Succeed in Business without Really Trying* and *I Can Get It for You Wholesale*, with little variation in the conflict between traditional work values and the free spirit and the triumph of the independent rogue operating in a world of modern working slaves. The staying power of these farces becomes even more evident if one considers how often they are revived in schools and local theaters. As shallow as they are, they seem to touch a responsive chord with white-collar audiences, who will probably supply a market for the office farce as long as they are hemmed in by the bureaucracies in which they work and are unfulfilled by the work they do.

Closely related in theme to the office farce, although possessed of a very different social stance, is Philip Barry's popular 1928 comedy *Holiday. Holiday* offers the comforting thesis that wealthy people who work too hard and earn too much money are unhappy, bored, and spiritually undernourished.[13] Johnny Case, a self-made New York attorney and an astonishingly shrewd investor, falls in love with Julia Seton, daughter of the "very very rich" (and very old riche) Edward Seton. They plan to marry, but quarrel irreconcilably over Johnny's anticapitalistic approach to life: he wants to take the money he has made in the stock market, quit work for a number of years, and try to find out who he is ("I don't want too much money"). His fiancée, very much her father's daughter, vehemently disagrees: "I've known men who don't work—and of all the footling, unhappy existences. . . . There's no thrill in the world like making money."[14] She receives predictable support from her father ("I consider his whole attitude deliberately unAmerican"). Johnny finally "gets" the girl, even though the girl is Linda, Julia's sister, who shares

Johnny's disdain for the shallow materialism and Chekhovian boredom that mark the life of the aristocracy.

This comedy, like the office farce, depicts the triumph of the self-made man who can be financially successful without losing his down-to-earth folksiness. And, in its shallow caricatures of "the rich," it fits squarely into that apparently inexhaustible literary tradition of heavy-handed satirization of the movers and shakers of the earth. Yet, unlike the farce, *Holiday* does offer a serious alternative to the ambitious and "productive" life—even for those possessed of the opportunity and talents to succeed, and succeed well. Johnny argues for a life of leisure, a life in which work is seen as a means of purchasing time away from work. As we have seen, historians such as Daniel Rodgers and David Riesman are convinced that a similar view of work has replaced the work ethic in the twentieth century for most American workers. Perhaps in no other modern American drama does this view find so strong an endorsement as it does in the lighthearted but seriously intended social statement in *Holiday*.

Through the 1930s the entertainment dramas that examined the American work ethic or the American work place were, by and large, plays of unabashed escapism or sentiment, venturing into the realm of social statement when social statement was conducive to the entertainment value at hand (such as it is in *Let's Get Rich*) or altogether unavoidable (as it is in *Hope for a Harvest*). What distinguishes such social statement from the social drama associated with the left-wing playwrights of the period is, by definition, the leftist playwrights' single-minded intention to change minds and change society in accordance with left-wing principles by the use of dramatic action revolving around specific social issues:

> The social dramatist encourages [positive action] . . . not only does he submit to external conditions but he must if necessary, help to change them. . . . He is, for the most part, unwilling to dedicate his work to mere pleasantries designed for mental and emotional adolescents.[15]

To be sure, in the 1930s the most forceful social commentary about the American work place was rendered by a number of left-wing, crusading playwrights whose period of productivity coincides closely with the depression years, 1929–1939. Self-consciously aware of the increasing turmoil among American blue-collar workers and their employers, the radical playwrights created dramas of socialist realism, a dramatic genre born out of the increasing left-wing activity of labor unions and the staggering number of unemployed or underemployed factory workers and miners in the East.[16] The persistence and proliferation of these plays and the groups that performed them (mostly in New York) gradually led to the acceptance of left-wing-oriented social drama for the "legitimate stage" by such "legitimate" playwrights as Elmer Rice, Sidney Kingsley, Sidney Howard, and Lillian Hellman.

The radical labor play and, in fact, the radical theater itself had inauspicious beginnings. In 1930 the earliest of the radical communist theater troups, The Workers Laboratory Theater and the Theater Collective, began staging crude, outdoor "happenings" called agitprops in an effort to recruit converts to the Communist Party. Possessed of nothing that could pass for quality, maturity, or theater professionalism, these skits consisted of "characters" and audience plants spouting left-wing rhetoric while an evil, mustachioed capitalist pantomimed dastardly capitalist deeds.

Such embarrassing productions could only serve to incite the already converted (and the extraordinarily patient converted at that). Even such radical journals as the *Daily Worker* and *The New Masses*, publications known to excuse a lot of bad art for the sake of ideology and damn a lot of good art in the name of bourgeois sentimentality, demanded more sophisticated scripts and production.[17] The sponsoring Communist Party and its splinter labor groups heard the message and by the middle 1930s The Workers Laboratory Theater and Theater Collectives had collapsed and had been replaced by theater groups with an interest in left-wing social drama that was written and performed to current professional standards. Among these new groups were the New Theater League, New Theater Union, and the Group Theater.[18]

Although current theatrical standards included plays of social realism, many radical labor plays maintained some stylistic ties to the early agitprops, which had the appeal of generating a conversion catharsis among the audience (or of making an attempt at it). Owing as much to black revival meetings and minstrel shows as to the primitive street skits of the Theater Collective and the Workers Laboratory Theater, the agitprop plays of the middle and late 1930s included some direct form of audience participation: planted actors in the audience, speeches directed to the audience, or some other shocking and generally antirealist, call-to-action technique.

The most elaborate example of this genre is Elmer Rice's *We, the People,* but a more modest and more typical example is *The Earth Is Ours,* written by William Kozlenko and produced by the New Theater League in 1937. Beginning as a realistic drama, the play opens on the story of Joe and Anna Sropa, a Polish immigrant couple whose farm is about to be taken away by a large company that wants to build a trolley line through the farm. Representatives from the company persuade the local police to pressure Sropa into selling his land for a ridiculously low price. But one night a confrontation between the police and the Sropas gets out of hand, resulting in the shooting death of Anna Sropa.

In the final scene of the play, Anna's funeral, a preacher speaks directly to the audience, which, as friends and peers, has become part of the cast as mourners at Anna's funeral. The preacher's eulogy is interrupted when a neighbor leaps to the forum and exhorts the guests-audience to rise up against the forces of big business and cooperating governments that oppress working people:

Anna did not die in vain. Her death has brought us all closer together. She has made us see the danger and the light. We know the men who murdered her will go free but they are guilty![19]

A variation on this highly melodramatic ending to be found in several of the more militant labor plays is the staging of a violent confrontation between workers and capitalists. Strongly reminiscent of the peasant uprising scene in Hauptmann's *The Weavers*, workers in Sklar's *Stevedore* and Hughes's *Scottsboro Ltd.* storm onto the stage shouting, yelling, and driving off the scabs, police, and allies of the capitalists. In more restrained plays, such as Blitzstein's *The Cradle Will Rock* or Ben Bengal's *Plant in the Sun*, a hubbub is created in the wings, and a handful of workers and proletariats on stage look out the window and lead the audience in cheering the "thousands of workers" gathering outside.

Because the direct address to the audience, the on-stage violence, and the off-stage gathering hordes were all intended to move an audience to immediate, direct political action, the successful agitprop drama portrayed the American working man and the problems of American labor as issues of the heart rather than of the head. Reflecting the radical view that the workers of America would join the class struggle through something more closely resembling religious conversion than political persuasion, the best of the agitprop writers built into their plays a fast pace and a lot of noise. The contrasting styles and equally contrasting popularity of Rice's *We, the People* and Odets's *Waiting for Lefty* are a case in point. Rice's play is unequivocally the most thoughtful, the most complex, and the most intellectually adventurous of the call-to-action plays of the 1930s, which is probably why it failed in the theater. Rice was willing to sacrifice pace and energy for content. But *Waiting for Lefty*, probably the most successful and historically the most important of the agit-props, aimed for its audience's heart and not its head.

Benefiting from Rice's ideas of uniting a variety of left-wing issues that surround a strike and setting up a radical meeting as part of a story line, Odets may well have benefited even more from Rice's mistaken attempt to rouse an audience to political action by elaborate, rational persuasion.

Opening in a strike meeting, in which each member of the audience becomes a member of a cab driver's union, *Waiting for Lefty* consists of six brief episodes that explain how a cab driver, a doctor, and an actor have all come to the strike meeting that night to declare their solidarity with the strikers and to denounce the system that simultaneously oppresses and unites all working people. The flashback episodes, which are scenes of "fourth-wall realism," alternate with scenes in the strike hall—scenes that grow in their intensity and potential violence with each "cut" to the flashbacks. The alternating of scenes keeps the audience on edge yet effectively directs all of its emotional energy to the final call-to-action scene in the strike hall:

> Agate. Hear it, boys. Hear it. Hell listen to me! Coast to coast! HELLO AMERICA! HELLO! WE'RE STORM-BIRDS OF THE WORKING-CLASS. WORKERS OF THE WORLD . . . OUR BONES AND BLOOD. And when we die they'll know what we did to make a new world! Christ, cut us up to little pieces. We'll die for what is right! Put fruit trees where our ashes are! (*To audience*) Well, what's the answer?
> All. Strike.
> Agate. LOUDER.
> All. STRIKE.
> Agate and others on stage. AGAIN.
> All. STRIKE STRIKE.[20]

If *We, the People* established the fact that radical labor drama had potential as important drama, *Waiting for Lefty* fulfilled that potential. Although it was well received by the press, the play is best remembered for the impact it made upon its opening-night audience:

> The first scene had not played two minutes when a shock
> of delighted recognition struck the audience like a tidal
> wave. . . . Line after line brought applause, whistles,
> bravos and heartfelt shouts of kinship.[21]

No other writer of 1930s agitprop drama (including Elmer
Rice, Langston Hughes, Paul Green, and William Kozlenko) was able to pull off this kind of success.

Clurman and others have attributed the success of
Lefty to Odets's lower-middle-class urban background, im-
plying that writers such as Rice, Green, and Lawson were
prevented from writing agitprop as effectively because of
their middle-class and upper-middle-class backgrounds.
But at least some credit is due Odets's understanding of the
dynamics of improvisation and the call-and-response elements in the agitprop theater and the black-inspired theatrical formats from which it grew. In the "Notes for
Production" on *Lefty*, Odets writes:

> The background of the episodes, a strike meeting, is not
> an excuse. Each of the committeemen shows in his episode
> the crucial moment of his life which brought him to the
> very platform. The dramatic structure on which the
> play is built is simple but highly effective. The form is
> the old black-face minstrel form of chorus, endmen,
> specialty men, and interlocutor.[22]

The radical agitprop dramas shared the burden of
presenting socially meaningful drama with a large number
of plays written in a strictly realistic mode. While advancing similar political positions, these realistic dramas
tended to be more cerebral and less impassioned than the
radical agitprops. The writers of these more strictly realistic dramas were concerned with many of the same issues
and themes as writers of radical drama—so much so that
Paul Green, Elmer Rice, and Clifford Odets wrote both
types of dramas and suffered little for their ventures into
a more conventional dramatic mode. Regarding work as
a social issue, realistic plays tended to explain the importance of work to men in a society where work was scarce

as opposed to the radical dramas, which advocated immediate takeover of the system of production by workers. Criticisms of capitalism and management practices were often explicit, but these plays tended to seek reform rather than revolution.

Of particular interest to the realist dramatists as well as the agitprop dramatists was the theme and setting of the strike and its accompanying conflicts between capital and labor, between work and family loyalties, and between group and individual prosperity. Perhaps the most important function of virtually all strike dramas, radical or reforming, was to argue the case for the economic and moral legitimacy of unions and union activity. Fully aware of the anti-American, pro-Communist stigma attached to labor unions in the days of the IWW protests against America's involvement in World War I, the authors of strike dramas took great pains to demonstrate that the American laborer could want to strike and want to be a union member and still be a decent, patriotic, and hardworking American. As a consequence, many strike dramas depict a conversion process in which a worker (or even someone sympathetic to workers, such as a liberal college professor) who only wants to be left alone is finally forced to join a union because of the rising tide of events and the increasingly desperate circumstances of his comrades. As he comes to the decision, the hero, in a climactic scene, swears allegiance to both his country and his union and joins the strike. Such conversion scenes are to be found, with little variation, in Lawson's *Marching Song*, Green's *The Enchanted Maze*, Odets's *Waiting for Lefty*, Rice's *We, the People*, Blitzstein's *The Cradle Will Rock*, and Bengal's *Plant in the Sun*. Yet no play spoke so passionately of the legitimacy of a worker's union loyalty in the face of conflicting interests as did Albert Maltz's *Black Pit*, a 1935 play of historical realism set in the coal-mining camps of West Virginia.

Joe Kavarsky, a Serb miner, returns to his family in a coal camp after spending three years in jail for strike activity. His pregnant wife earns pennies by doing laundry for other mining families. His wife's brother, who lives with them, is confined to a wheel chair because of a mining accident and cannot work. As a blackballed striker, Joe has no prospects of earning any money in the camps until the mine owner, worried about new strike activity, offers Joe his old mining job back plus a bonus if he will agree to report to him any new strike activity that may be going on.

Reluctant to betray his fellow miners, Joe decides to play both sides by taking the money but giving the owner misleading and insignificant information. Joe's plan succeeds until the death of a miner in a gas-filled part of the mine causes enough strike talk to reach the boss's attention independently of Joe's misleading reports.

Joe is confronted by the boss, who orders him to name the strike organizer or to be barred from this and any other coal mine in the state. Joe, fearing for the health of his wife and baby, gives the boss the name of the man. Naturally, the immediate disappearance of the strike organizer calls the other miners' attentions to Joe's traitorous activities. Joe pleads his case to his fellow miners, citing his pregnant wife, his crippled brother-in-law, and his lack of alternatives. But Maltz returns the harsh verdict in the voice of Joe's crippled brother-in-law himself:

> No, Jesus Cris', you be lie. I no be lak you. I gone sleep on groun'. I gone eat coal, I gone die from starve' fore I cheat on odern miner. You want to be stool pigeon? Okay. (*He spits.*) I no gone stay in same house wit' stool pigeon.[23]

Individually and collectively, strike dramas clearly tried to establish a work ethic of their own: while working at an honest job was necessary for a good and virtuous life, loyalty to one's fellow workers was at least as necessary. If they never succeeded in convincing anyone that joining a union should be made one of the sacraments, the series of labor martyrs, traitors, loyalists, converts, and hale-fellows-well-met who paraded through these strike dramas certainly reflected (although they probably did not influence) the labor movement's own recurring interest in gaining social respectability among the American people.[24]

Because of that desire to gain for workers the respect and sympathy of the American people, the left-wing realist and agitprop dramatists of the thirties rarely strayed too far from the most traditional, even clichéd, expressions of pre-industrial Puritan work values in their dramas, and particularly in plays about unemployment.[25] A recurring theme throughout the 1930s, the extolling of the dignity and purposefulness of work, was central to the left-wing dramatist's plea (demand) for an end to unemployment and his protest against management coercion of labor by threats of firings and lockouts. Moreover, unemployment was seen as a source of emasculation, cutting down the American male in the eyes of his wife, girlfriend, or family, and making of him a vulnerable, sympathetic figure.

In what comes as close to an Elizabethan soliloquy as the social drama of the thirties could produce, there is a moment in many labor plays in which the theme of dignity and purpose through work is articulated by a major or minor character who "stops the show" (to say nothing of his normal conversation) to express his need for work. From the reluctant union convert in Lawson's *Marching Song* comes:

> I lay there on the couch last night, watchin' the stars through the holes in the roof. It's a hell of a place to lay all night thinkin'. I ain't a Bolshevik, but my kid needs milk. . . . I don't know what the hell went wrong. I done skilled work right here for ten years. . . . if we can't go back where do we go. Christ, let a man die if he's got no place to go.[26]

Uncle Benny, the janitor at the university in Paul Green's *The Enchanted Maze*, teaches a radical student a lesson about work and the common man:

A man's got to have something in his life—something to
do. Something he can call his'n, his work. (*Fondling his
broom*) You know, I love this old broom. And everytime
I have to get a new one, it hurts me, I save 'em all, put
'em away in a closet like buried soldiers. Yes sir I love
my brooms for they're the heart of my job.[27]

And Adamec, the crippled factory worker who is dependent upon his two sons in Leopold Atlas's *But for the Grace
of God*, gives us:

Relief! I make a buck, two a week doing odd jobs. Can't
get on relief. And who the hell wants relief anyway. I got
two hands I want to work. I want to do something.[28]

Not surprisingly, Adamec's disdain for relief is a common
sentiment expressed in these plays as a way of re-enforcing
the respect that labor people and the suspect left have for
traditional work values. The message in many of these
plays is that the American laborer is an upright, hardworking family man who wishes only to make something of
himself.

Interestingly enough, several playwrights of the thirties were sensitive to the effects of poverty on a man's
sexual self-image—an idea that we associate with the socio-
logical research of the late 1960s and 1970s. Hard times
in a labor drama often lead to tensions in a man's relationship with his wife or lover as well as to difficulties caused
by the emasculation of a father. The collapse or threat of
collapse of families is evident in such unemployment
dramas as *Waiting for Lefty, We, the People, But for the
Grace of God, Bluestone Quarry* and Lashing and Has-
ting's *Class of '29* (1936), as well as in less strident dramas
such as *Hope for a Harvest, Tenant Farmers,* and Fred
Eastman's *Bread* (1927). Not unlike Persis and Silas Lapham in Sabine's play, the principals sometimes manage
to resolve the conflict of work and family. For example, in
Waiting for Lefty, Edna, an embittered wife, withholds
her respect from her husband Joe until he joins the cab

drivers' union. As she tries to convince him to join, she tells him flatly that his failure to suport the union's strike effort has made of him an inadequate husband, father, and sex partner. Joe agrees and runs eagerly to the union hall, anxious to regain his dignity and his domestic tranquility.

On the other hand, love and sex are sometimes made the victim of hard times, underscoring the left's intensive desire to see an end to unemployment. Oddly enough, however, a profoundly antifemale disposition creeps into a number of these plays, which portray the hero as being trapped hopelessly between the demands of his woman and the demands of his work. This theme is quite pronounced in Lawson's *Marching Song*, in which a skilled factory worker, Peter Russell, decides to leave a secure job for a better paying but less secure one because his wife insists that they save up enough money to buy a house. When Russell loses his new job, Lawson appears to join him in blaming the woman for the couple's predicament. Although the couple is reunited when Russell's union is successful, Lawson never fully excuses the woman for getting her husband into considerable trouble in the first place.

Other plays have vicious, gratuitous criticisms of wives and lovers of men out of work. In *Class of '29*, a woman plans with her father-in-law to get her husband free of the ego-deflating dependency he has on handouts from his father. They set up the husband in a job with a company that has no need for him but pays him "a salary" that comes from payments the father is secretly making to the company. When the husband discovers the ploy, he is understandably angry at his wife, but the degree to which he verbally assaults her (and all women) and the fact that the ruse demolishes the marriage forever seems a bit excessive:

> Ken. It takes a woman to do a thing like that.
> Laura. I love you.
> Ken. It takes love. That's what love is. That's what it does to a man. And when I was a boy I wondered why the world's wisest men hung out with whores.[29]

In *But for the Grace of God* similar evidence of gratuitous antifemale hostility comes out in a dialogue between a young, underpaid factory worker and his girlfriend, who has no other function in the play but to meet him in one scene and receive his unprovoked abuse:

> Rosey. If my old man were alive, my sister would have stayed at home'n I wouldn't need to work. I'd go to school 'n maybe be a teacher.
> Josey. (with a malicious bark) Teacher! quit dreamin' dat crap all your life. You know what you'll become when you grow up . . . a whore![30]

There is no question that the extent of the hostility revealed in these scenes is designed to show the degree of bitterness and misery that festers among working-class people who are unemployed and/or impoverished. Moreover, the inclusion of a family life in the dramatization of labor problems was clearly an attempt on the part of the new "mature" social drama to overcome its crude beginnings and enter the world of serious dramatic art.[31] Yet between the heavy-handed husband-wife-union solidarity of *Waiting for Lefty* and the misdirected hostility of men emasculated by poverty in *Class of '29* and *But for the Grace of God* there is (except in *We, the People*) little evidence that the labor dramatists were able effectively to handle the work/family balance they sought. Seeming to distract the authors from the business at hand (the problems of working people and their work), the balance of work and family values that was to become very important to Miller, Williams, and others saw little important artistic development in the left-wing drama of the 1930s despite valiant attempts by several authors.

The stark economic conditions of the 1930s demanded that any social dramatist who dealt with the life and work of blue-collar workers portray these characters as vulnerable if not victimized by the depression. There seemed to be no argument on any front that the lot of the common laborer, both in his home and on the job, was determined largely by the relative amount of misfortune that befell his factory, farm, mine, or union during that dismal era. What social dramatists were not so certain about was how the professional—the professor, doctor, lawyer—fit into the trials of the times. The professional might be just another working stiff in the capitalist machinery, a hero of the aspiring middle class, or a being wholly removed and exempt from the strains of life in hard times. Even authors who held similar views on the plight of the common laborer had markedly differing views on the nature of professional work during the 1930s.

For example, a stark contrast in the portrayal of the medical profession can be seen in the difference between Sidney Kingsley's portrayal of doctors in *Men in White* (1933) and Clifford Odets's portrayal of doctors in *Waiting for Lefty*. Kingsley, a hard-nosed reformer of the realist school (*Dead End*), was apparently so enamored with the jargon and technology surrounding modern medicine that, at the height of the depression, he wrote a play of virtually unrestrained doctor-worship, "documenting" the trials of the "men in medicine who dedicate themselves with quiet heroism to man." The men in white struggle against profit-oriented hospital administrators, wealthy hypochondriacs who demand pampering, and ethical crises such as whether or not to take an immensely profitable position in private practice or to remain at the hospital and live a life of mere affluence. Kingsley also embues the play with several explanatory footnotes that define the medical jargon in the script; these statements permit him to wax progressive on medicine in America:

> Dr. Rongey, former president of the A.M.A., estimates that there are more illegal abortions every year in New York and Chicago than there are children actually born in those cities. Most of these operations are performed on otherwise respectable, law-abiding married women. Proof enough that here is another social problem that can't be eliminated by legislation. . . . A saner healthier attitude is the one adopted by the Soviet government

which is fostering birth control education and instituting legal abortion clinics.[32]

As Bonin and others have noted, the play is the blueprint for those countless films, plays, and soap operas that engage in mythmaking about doctors and hospitals and that portray the medical profession as a world complete unto itself, removed entirely from what Samuel Johnson would call the "lights and noises of the common day."

In *Lefty*, however, the real world intrudes upon the medical profession with a vengeance. A young surgeon, Dr. Benjamin, is not permitted to perform an operation on a senator's son. When he asks his supervisor, Dr. Barnes, for an explanation he learns that his entire career is in jeopardy because of class distinctions (senators' sons get upper-class surgeons), anti-Semitism (the board of directors of the hospital does not like Jewish doctors), financial crises (declining donations are forcing the closing of several hospital charity wings and the subsequent laying off of medical personnel), and the bumbling stupidity of the system itself ("Doctors don't run medicine in this country. The men who know their jobs don't run anything here"). All of this moves Dr. Benjamin to join the class struggle in order to free all oppressed workers. Invoking his proletarian roots, a clear reminder from Odets that the loftiest of professionals is not far removed from the commonest of laborers, Benjamin renounces his profession and swears allegiance to the class struggle in America:

> My parents gave up an awful lot to get me this far. They ran a little drygoods shop in the Bronx until their pitiful little savings went in the crash last year. . . . Many things these radicals say. . . . You don't believe theories until they happen to you. . . . What future's ahead, I don't know. Get some job to keep alive—and study and work and learn my place—Fight! maybe get killed but goddam! We'll go ahead.[33]

During the depression era, the lawyer was not quite as controversial among the social dramatists as was the doctor. Attorneys were mostly confined to the courtroom-mystery entertainments that, although they tended to portray lawyers as shrewd and glib, were not concerned with presenting a picture of their actual work. While Rice's *Counselor-at-Law* raised questions about how unfulfilling a lawyer's life can be (see discussion of Rice in Chapter 2), escapist mysteries, such as DeLeon's *The Silent Witness* (1936) were more typical of the lawyer's lot in depression-era dramas.

Educators, on the other hand, seemed to many social dramatists to be ripe for a radical conversion. In addition to the radicalizing of professors and teachers in *We, the People* and Green's *The Enchanted Maze*, Sklar and Maltz's *Peace on Earth* saw professors move from studied neutrality to firm commitment to the social revolution.

With professionals either removed entirely from the revolutionary doctrines of the left wing or placed directly in the center of the class struggle, it is not surprising to find at least one playwright using a professional as the voice of moderation in the midst of political strife, and so it was with pharmacist Jim Cogswell, the hero of George Brewer's *Tide Rising* (1937). More a liberal on principle than a liberal on issues, Brewer sought in his drama to "balance the coverage" of labor disputes by contemporary dramatists who had been overwhelmingly left-wing and antibusiness in their biases:

> The story of *Tide Rising* deals microcosmically with labor troubles of America. Other plays have dealt with the same theme, but with this difference: they have for the most part presented a picture of industrial strife from the point of view of exploited labor. They have been written in a crusading spirit and frequently with a strong "liberal bias." (I know of no labor play yet written which treats the problem from a point of view sympathetic toward the noble industrialist victimized by unconscionable labor agitators and sit-down strikers, though that way is wide open for some ambitious playwright. . . . I attempted in *Tide Rising* to write a sociological play

which cried a plague on both houses. In it I endeavored to show that both extremists are so blindly engaged in a battle for power, one endeavoring to hold it, the other attempting to seize it, that both contemptuously trample on the general welfare and upon the vast number of people who disbelieve in their extreme and intemperate ambitions.[34]

To give voice to this "vast number of people" Brewer could have done no better than to choose a small-town pharmacist. Cogswell is "part business" in that he owns a pharmacy and wields a modest amount of political power as a member of the town council. On the other hand, he is also part "common man"; he is at the mercy of a ruthless drug wholesaler who dispenses and withholds vital supplies on the basis of Jim's sales receipts. Moreover, he is dependent upon the good will of the town's factory workers who frequent his drug store. Finally, as a small businessman, he is as much his own wage slave as he is his own boss.

Cogswell becomes caught in the middle of a labor dispute in the local factory because the factory owner, Graham Hay, is a friend of his and because the strike leader, Ruth, is his daughter-in-law. As the tide of events rises, Hay and Ruth become increasingly irrational and violent in their demands; Hay refuses to offer a competitive or livable wage while Ruth will not negotiate for anything less than worker control of the factory. Hay finally brings in a platoon of strikebreakers and police to open the factory while Ruth organizes her workers to confront them violently. With the tiny town facing war in the streets, Cogswell lures Hay and Ruth into a meeting, locks them in a room, and tells them that they cannot come out until they have reached an agreement. As he departs, Cogswell extols the virtue of the middle way in the conflict of labor and management:

> You and everyone like you all over this land, do you know what you are doing? You're going to destroy the country. You're going to drive us to communism or fascism. But

you've done something for me. You've shown me the answer I've been looking for. I'm in the clear now. I know where I stand. You'll destroy my democracy will you? We men who still have faith in reason and fair play. You haven't counted on us; We've been forgotten in your wrangling. Now we're going to be heard from.[35]

Clearly Brewer sees the pharmacist as the political, intellectual, economic, and moral center of the nation; he is not as wealthy as a doctor, nor as intellectual as a teacher, nor as shrewd as an attorney. He is a man to be admired but not to be in awe of. As a self-made man in a small town, Cogswell easily embodies the apolitical values of family, independence, and hard work (which for Brewer is a profoundly nonpolitical issue) that stand as a shield against the political pressures of the world that assault him from the right and left. As a character of heroic neutrality rather than heroic action, Cogswell is *Our Town*'s George Webb transplanted into the picket lines of the thirties and coming through with his values intact.

By and large the American work place in the drama of the 1920s and 1930s was portrayed in the familiar genres and styles that we have examined thus far in this chapter: realistic entertainments, comedies, and left-wing social dramas, which are "familiar" because of the amount of attention they have received from scholars of dramatic literature. But some less familiar dramatic experiments also dealt with work themes and, by virtue of their unconventional manner of presentation, lent some minor variation to the work-related themes we have already seen.

In addition to *The Adding Machine*, the expressionist school gave to American drama O'Neill's *The Hairy Ape* (1921), probably the most widely read American expressionist play. *The Hairy Ape* is the bizarre odyssey of a Neanderthal-like ship's coal stoker, who undertakes a self-destructive search for his identity after being told by an aristocratic young woman that "he is a beast." The search reveals gradually the man's, and presumably modern man's, dehumanized state on two curious and seemingly incongruous levels—he is apelike, but he is also machinelike:

> See de steel work? Steel, dat's me. Youse guys live on it and tink you're somep'n. But I'm in it, see! I'm de hoistin' engine dat makes it go up! I'm it—de inside and bottom of it. . . .[36]

In a sense, Yank's identification with his machine is comparable to Silas Lapham's identification with his paint ("It was my blood"), although the ramifications of the tension it causes between Yank and his own humanity are something quite apart (and something quite rare in modern American drama) from the tensions that evolve between Lapham's work values and his family values.

What does recur in later dramas that first appeared as a motif in this and other expressionist plays is the irrepressible visual and aural presence of "the machine." The bulks of the furnaces and boilers outlined menacingly in the background of the stokehole scene in *The Hairy Ape* and the "tumult of noise" that opens the play are likely sources for the mechanical motifs in *Marching Song, Hope for a Harvest, But for the Grace of God.*

The most curious dramatic experiment of the 1920s did not come from the expressionists but instead from the rather grand vision of John Howard Lawson. In his comedy *Processional* (1925), Lawson sought to establish a particularly American dramatic idiom to handle particularly American themes, such as a coal-mining strike in West Virginia (the subject, more or less, of this very loosely structured work). The source for this American idiom was to be vaudeville:

> I have endeavored to create a method as far removed from the older realism or the facile mood of Expressionism. It is apparent that this new technique is essentially vaudevillesque in character . . . a development of the rich vitality of the two-a-day revue and the musical extravaganza.[37]

Indeed, the play contains recognizable vaudevillian types: the Jewish low comedian, the hard-boiled officer of the law, the slick city journalist, as well as an on-stage band that lurks behind the principal characters, waiting to pounce on anything that remotely resembles a song cue. But if a coal-mining strike was suitable material for slapstick and rimshots in 1925, it was entirely unsuitable shortly thereafter. Depression-era issues such as strikes and poverty soon became serious and lent themselves quite easily to the restrictions of the "older realism" as well as the "facile mood of Expressionism." Lawson's theory was probably sound, but his timing was terrible.

An intriguing, although short-lived, experiment in American dramatic literature of the 1930s was the Living Newspapers, which were the controversial products of Hallie Flanagan's Federal Theater Project. Federal Theater was primarily a production program—or several production units, to be more precise—that produced classics of the theater as well as contemporary plays written by people who were not on the Federal Theater staff. However, the Federal Theater staff actually devised this clever art form that combined propaganda, government documents, news reports, and editorials to make what can be loosely called a playscript.

The controversy surrounding the Living Newspapers parallels the controversies surrounding the Federal Theater Project as a whole, which was severely criticized by journalists and conservative congressmen. These critics contended that the entire project was merely a forum for left-wing, and particularly pro-Roosevelt, economic and political policies under the guise of an employment program for actors, playwrights, directors, and theater technicians. In truth, it was both. While some supporters of Federal Theater denied the charges of the conservatives, others boasted of the pervasiveness of propaganda in the plays and of the cleverness employed by Federal Theater in embuing its productions with left-wing ideology. In

1937 Wilson Whitman wrote gleefully of a children's production of *The Emperor's New Clothes* that contained a plea from oppressed, exploited weavers working on the royal robes. He also notes that the Federal Theater's first ballet production, *Dance of Death*, contained an allegorical condemnation of the British bourgeoisie that escaped conservative critics completely.[38]

Not surprisingly, the project's own scripts grew out of and reflected similar political viewpoints and biases. The format of the Living Newspaper—a play dramatizing a single pressing social issue—is generally credited to Elmer Rice, who, as a friend of Hallie Flanagan, was among the first persons she called to head up a major unit of the Federal Theater (and who, on the other hand, as a less-than-patient negotiator of the federal bureaucracy, was among the first major figures to abandon the project). The actual task of writing the Living Newspapers fell to a group of staff members of the Federal Theater led by Arthur Arent.

The Living Newspapers served several functions simultaneously. First, they allowed Flanagan to assign parts to many actors, sometimes as many as sixty actors in a single production. Secondly, the Living Newspaper allowed Flanagan to pursue her lifetime interest in experimental theater production and, particularly, her recently acquired interest in European epic theater production. Like the epic plays of Brecht, the Living Newspapers sought to regale their audiences with a particular stance rather than reveal to them some subjective truth about the human condition. Moreover, the staging of the Living Newspapers borrowed heavily from epic theater practices, such as the flashing of headlines and slogans on a screen and the inclusion of lectures and speeches to the audiences as part of the drama.

Finally, born as they were of New Deal ideology, Living Newspapers did indeed provide Flanagan and her people with an oportunity to explore some of the serious social issues of the day, including the corruption of the judicial system (*1935*), racial discrimination (*Liberty Deferred*), and, in the most famous and most successful of the Living Newspapers, the critical shortage of housing in America (*One-Third of a Nation*).[39]

Naturally, problems of work, labor, and unemployment were also treated in Living Newspaper scripts and produced with the experimental, sophisticated techniques of epic theater. For example, in *Triple-A Ploughed Under* (1936) the plight of the American farmer during the depression was documented with readings and summaries of news stories and Department of Agriculture statistics. Moreover, the play made a largely successful attempt to show the economic cause-and-effect relationships between dropping farm income and unemployment in East-coast factories—a socioeconomic argument that was "brought home" by the effective device of having farmers and factory workers standing on either side of the stage in the final scene, shouting to one another, "We need you." In *Power* (1937) the demonstration of the power that a large company has over the small farmer or the small, independent businessman was similar to the themes protesting private property that are found in plays such as *Tenant Farmers* or *The Earth Is Ours*. But the Living Newspaper presented a quasi-academic battery of suport for its position, dramatizing situations, summaries, and even direct quotes from relevant journalistic and research publications.

Although academic interest in the Living Newspapers has grown since the discovery of the lost production records of the Federal Theater Project in an airplane hangar in 1974, their influence upon the theater seems to be limited to the period of the New Deal itself, and their influence on American playwrighting seems to be nonexistent. Moreover, inasmuch as they sought in large measure to demonstrate pro-Roosevelt positions, their contribution to the ideological and political complexion of American drama is rather limited as well.

Work and the Work Ethic

Although hardly united in purpose, point of view, artistic technique, or political persuasion, the dramatists who used work themes in their plays during the 1920s and 1930s had, by and large, a common goal and common purpose: to examine the ethics, the values, and the meaning of work in light of the "new realities" of the modern work place—the union, mechanization, the bureaucratized big business, the burgeoning class of office workers, and the immigrant common laborer. Moreover, through most of these plays, ranging from the most radical to the most conservative and from the most experimental to the most traditional, comes a sincere and serious plea for dignity through work. Whether that dignity is to come from keeping one's youth and spontaneity in the midst of the office rat race (as it is in the office farce), from joining one's working brothers on the job in wresting power away from the bosses (as it is in the left-wing labor drama), by individuals committing themselves to pre-industrial virtues of hard work and self-discipline (as it is in sentimental dramas), or whether dignity is lost forever in confrontations with the machine (as it is in expressionist drama), the quest for dignity through work was a powerful guiding force in the proliferation and variety of work themes in American drama of those two decades and beyond. The plays reflect the economic paradox of the period, a combination of the expansion of the machinery and systems of work and a widespread unavailability of work. Their playwrights sought to teach their audiences how to create their own humanity and find a sense of belonging in a modern world of work that offered neither.

IV

WORK AND
THE SECOND WORLD WAR

By the late 1930s events in Europe pointed to an inevitable American involvement in the European conflict. America's military, political, economic, and psychological preparation for that involvement drew the nation's attention away from strikes, unemployment, and the other major social issues of the depression years. Most historians credit America's preparation for and subsequent involvement in the war with actually ending the depression. Indeed, the end of the thirties coincided with increased productivity, a drop in unemployment in the major urban areas, stepped-up conscription, and other signs that an active economy was relieving the economic and psychological burdens.[1]

This change in America's economic well-being and political priorities was reflected clearly in the changes that occurred in the serious drama written during and immediately following World War II. After 1939, virtually no new "garden variety" left-wing labor plays appeared in print or on stage in major American productions; in fact, all of the major radical labor theater groups had collapsed by 1941.[2] Left-wing dramatists had turned much of their attention to the issues of anti-fascism and pacifism, while more moderate playwrights directed their attentions to various aspects of the war. What emerged from the drama of the 1940s was a substantial variety and number of war plays.

An examination of these plays reveals to us several recurring approaches to the war—approaches that formed the basis of the countless war movies and television programs that were produced from the late 1940s through the early 1960s. Among them are the drama of pure patriotism (Rouveral's *Young Man of Today* [1944], Moss Hart's *Winged Victory* [1943]), the thriller of military and underground intrigue set in Nazi-occupied Europe (James's *Winter Soldiers* [1943], Hellman's *Watch on the Rhine* [1941]), the grim, hard-edged portrait of men at war (Laurents's *Home of the Brave* [1945], Brown's *A Sound of Hunting* [1945]), and the farcical comedy of military highjinks (Behrman's *Jacobowski and the Colonel* [1944], Heggen and Logan's *Mr. Roberts* [1948]).

In their efforts to examine the infinite variety of tensions, experiences, and conditions that arise in the extraordinary circumstances of war, both serious and comic playwrights employed values and ideas that were familiar and meaningful to the civilian American playgoer, such as romantic love in the war zone, good versus evil, the battle for home and family, and the relationship of the war to the civilian world of work. It is this last theme that is central to our discussion here.

The most common connections between the war and the world of everyday work are found in plays that feature fighting men who refer to their soldiering as performing a normal job. The many playwrights who use this technique of characterization were in all likelihood influenced by the common practice among combat soldiers of referring to acts of extreme horror and violence in terms of normal work in an effort to cope with the extreme pressures that warfare places on a man. In fact, the practice of viewing warfare as just another job is presented in many plays as a soldier's defense mechanism by which he attempts to make the irrational and abnormal seem rational and normal so that he can accept the otherwise wholly unacceptable.

It is this expression of war as normal, routine work that forms the central theme of John Steinbeck's *The Moon Is Down* (1942). *The Moon Is Down* is a humanistic examination of a fictional Nazi occupation of a Norwegian mining town. The play, which was vigorously criticized for being too tolerant of the Nazis, portrays the conquered and the conquerer as victims of something that is larger than both of them. The central character, Nazi Colonel Lanser, sees his army's invasion as a normal enterprise in the everyday world of jobs and work. By explaining his acts of aggression against his victims in terms of only doing "his job," he seeks to minimize the emotional trauma for both his victims and himself. For example, when the colonel threatens to shoot the local mayor's cook for biting a soldier's hand, Lanser uses the "war as job" metaphor in an effort to tone down the cruelty in the threat without actually withdrawing it: "We just want to do our jobs. . . . Our instructions are to get along with your people. Please co-operate for the good of all."[3] The colonel takes the same approach when he executes one of the town's most popular young miners for killing a Nazi soldier in self-defense. The colonel's explanation to the mayor is an appeal from one "working man" to another to see this bloodshed and butchery as part of a normal, common, everyday line of work: "I am very sorry about this . . . I have a job to do. You surely recognize that."[4] The colonel even seeks to convince the town and himself that the citizens' lives are not being disrupted by the Nazi occupation because work in the mines will be proceeding as usual.

Ultimately, however, both the captor and the captured recognize that this rationalization is a failure in a final confrontation with the town's mayor, whom the colonel holds as a hostage against the townspeople's mounting hostility.

> The military, the political patterns I work in, has certain tendencies and practices which are invariable. . . . One of the tendencies of the military mind is an inability to learn, an inability to see beyond the killing which is its job.[5]

Steinbeck's view that it is an exercise in hypocrisy and self-deception to explain the horrors of war in terms of normal routine work is shared by other playwrights. In Arthur Laurents's *Home of the Brave*, a work best known for its handling of anti-Semitism, an army mapmaker named Coney is forced to leave a wounded buddy to die in a South Pacific foxhole so that the maps they had made could be delivered to army headquarters. Back in the states Coney suffers from guilt feelings over his responsibility in the death of his fellow soldier. He is counseled by an army psychologist who tries to comfort him by telling him that he had done his job and done it well:

> Coney. I should have stayed with him.
> Doctor. If you'd stayed with him, the maps would be lost. The maps were your job and the job comes first.[6]

Coney takes momentary comfort from this explanation, but, the analogy between job and war collapses under the weight of war's extraordinary pressures. Coney finally reveals that he is glad the man was killed; Coney explains that all men in war are happy when someone else gets killed because they are relieved that they have been spared. Through Coney, Laurents tells us that there is nothing in the familiar, comfortable, and ethical context of everyday work that can account for such an experience.

While Laurents and Steinbeck view the attempt to explain war in terms of work as a hollow rationalization, other playwrights see it as a legitimate means by which a fighting man can keep himself sane. It has for some playwrights a quasi-religious value in that it allows a man to find a purpose in an existence that might otherwise defy a man's attempt to discern meaning in it. Donald Bevan's *Stalag 17* (1948), a mystery drama about American soldiers in a Nazi POW camp, focuses on the soldiers' search for a Nazi informer in their midst. At one point in the investigation, some of the men speculate about why an American in a POW camp would spy on his buddies. The most articulate answer comes from Corporal Pierce, who is of course the yet-to-be discovered turncoat:

For him this is his job. It's easier for a man to live under these conditions as long as he has a purpose. To him this is his duty.[7]

In Moss Hart's *Winged Victory* (1943) we find the same need for a fighting man to see his participation in the war as a job in order for him to find a meaning in some of the war's horrors. Pilot Allan Ross is beset with grief over the shooting of two boyhood friends who were under his command. As Allan recalls their shared boyhood ambition to join the Air Force, a fellow pilot consoles him:

Allan. (as airplanes would pass overhead) we shouted, 'that's us in a little while.' Now Frankie's gone and maybe Pink.
Irving. Look, Al, it won't do any good to think like that. It doesn't help Pinky. This is his job and our job and we've got to finish it.
Allan. Yes. Yes, you're right Irv. If only—
Irving. If only what?
Allan. If only people learn something out of this. I don't want Frankie dead and Pinky blind for nothing.[8]

As in *Stalag 17*, there is an assumption in *Winged Victory* that the performance of a job is a moral necessity, and virtually anything that occurs in the dutiful performance of that job is an acceptable if not an ethical occurrence. (See footnote 4 on Arendt's theory of the "banality of evil.") For Allan and Irving, all that is moral and right about hard work is also moral and right about the war. For men who believe in the value of work, the concept of the war as work can serve as both a religion and a pipedream: it makes sense out of circumstances that might otherwise be unexplainable, and it provides comfort during war's unbearably stressful moments

The power of the war-as-a-job metaphor to detach a man from the intense emotional experiences of war was given a peculiar twist in Paul Osborn's *A Bell for Adano* (1944), a dramatic adaptation of John Hersey's novel. In

this play Maj. Victor Joppolo, an Italian-American assigned to supervise the allied occupation of the city Adano,
Italy, approaches his assignment with the detached, efficient manner of any white-collar executive assigned to a
specific administrative task: "I know my job. I know what
I want to do here." Immediately Joppolo assumes the trap-
pings of an executive on the job: a bombed-out building is
converted to his business office, complete with inner office
and outer office; he takes on Giuseppe, a local assistant who
calls Joppolo "Boss" rather than "Major"; paperwork and
conferees flow in and out of the office as if it were located
on Wall Street. At first Joppolo even speaks the language
of the efficient, task-oriented executive:

> I have been trying to get the ideas of various people as
> to what's the first thing to be done. I know that the peo-
> ple are hungry and that the streets need to be cleaned up.[9]

But just as the facade of the detached working man collapses under war's emotional reality in *The Moon Is
Down*, Joppolo's studied efficiency and executive preten-
sions dissolve when he develops a love for the people he is
assigned to supervise. Gradually he becomes less and less
the hard-driving executive and more and more "the lovely
American." He ignores army brass directives that might
disrupt the villagers' lives, he falls in love with one of the
women in the town, and he schemes to acquire from the
navy an iron bell to replace the town's symbol of life and
unity that had been destroyed by the Fascists prior to his
arrival. Whereas Lanser, Coney, Pierce, and Allan Ross
used the just-a-job approach to war in order to shield
themselves from its terrible emotional consequences, Joppolo used it to detach himself temporarily from the love
and tenderness he was to find as Adano's chief occupation
officer.

Whether they see their characters as hypocrites, manly
heroes, or closet sentimentalists, the playwrights who
develop the theme of the war as a job all share a similar
point of view about the nature of work per se. Specifically,

all of their characters who approach the war as a job do so in order to deaden their feelings—a fact that speaks to the degree to which mechanization and numbing routiniza-tion had taken hold of most American jobs by the 1940s. To them, and presumably to the audience, a job, whether confronted at war or at home, is something that must be approached by a man who is detached, wholly rational, intellectually facile, yet emotionally rigid. Under the ex-treme conditions of war, of course, dullness and detach-ment may be seen as mind-saving virtues. Colonel Lanser, Allan Ross, Victor Joppolo, and Corporal Pierce all as-sociate the loss of a normal job with the loss of purpose, and it is the loss of purpose that represents the greatest threat to the psychological well-being of war heroes in war dramas. So whether an author adopts the skeptical posi-tion of Steinbeck and Laurents or the patriotic sentiments of Hart and Osborn, he is acutely aware of the power of that sense of purpose that lies embedded in the familiar, if dull, and the comfortable, if routine, world of normal everyday work.

If the American playwright saw the combat soldier as a man who was desperate for the normal routine of work, he also saw the noncombatant as a man starved for the romance of wartime heroics as an escape from the routine of a real everyday job. In fact, the longing for mili-tary adventure as an escape from boredom with a civilian job is a major theme in some of the most notable plays of the war period, including Robert Sherwood's *The Rugged Path* (1945) and Heggen and Logan's *Mr. Roberts* (1948).

In *The Rugged Path*, forty-year-old newspaper editor Morey Vinion has serious doubts about his ability to measure up to the expectations and reputations of his late father-in-law, a legendary journalist from whom he "in-herited" his current position:

> I've seen some faint glimmering of light. Maybe it's deceptive but it's there. And what it's showing me is this: I've failed—I'm not the thing your father tried to create.[10]

Vinion leaves his prestigious position, his wife, and his middle-class household and becomes a cook on a destroyer in the South Pacific. While in the combat zone he discovers the meaningful work he could never find as a journalist. After a night of enemy bombardment, he speaks of the new life he relishes:

> [Then] I was a correspondent—an Olympian observer—stationed far above the battle. But last night I was just another Joe passing the ammunition. When those Jap planes came in low, I didn't think in terms of phrases.[11]

On the night before he dies in combat, Vinion gives final testimony to the resuscitation he has received after a life of meaningless work on the sidelines: "[The war] is a revival of the spirit, a restoration of the faith."

The theme of the war as an escape from and cure for the meaninglessness of everyday work also lies at the center of the most beloved play of the Second World War, *Mr. Roberts*. Lieutenant Junior Grade Doug Roberts is the second-in-command on a navy cargo ship that makes routine supply deliveries in a noncombat zone in the Pacific. Eager for a transfer to a war zone, Roberts is continuously thwarted by his ship's nameless captain, who needs Roberts's efficiency to maintain the ship's good service record and to assure his own imminent promotion and continued safe duty. Like Vinion, Roberts sees his work as routine and meaningless and thus sees his life as being equally meaningless. The combat transfer is Roberts's only hope for escape:

> I was up on the bridge . . . All of a sudden I noticed something. Little black specks crawling over the horizon. I looked through the glasses and it was a formation of our ships that stretched for miles. Carriers and battleships and cans—a whole task force, Doc . . . I could see the men on the bridges. And this is what knocked me out, Doc. Somehow—I thought I was on those bridges—I thought I was riding west across the Pacific. I watched them until they were out of sight, Doc—and I was right there on

> those bridges all the time . . . And then I looked down
> from our bridge and saw the Captain's palm tree.
> (*Points at palm tree, then bitterly.*) Our trophy for
> superior achievement. The Admiral John J. Finchley
> award for delivering more toothpaste and toilet paper
> than any other Navy cargo ship in the safe area of the
> Pacific.[12]

With the aid of some shenanigans from his comrades on
the ship, Roberts finally schemes successfully to get himself
transferred to a destroyer. In a letter to his former ship-
mates we learn that the flight from routine navy work to
heavy combat duty was for him the same soul-saving stroke
of good fortune that it was for Morey Vinion:

> I've been aboard this destroyer for two weeks now and
> we've already been through four air attacks. I'm in the
> war at last, Doc. I've caught up with the task force that
> passed me by. I'm glad to be here, I had to be here. But
> I'm thinking now of you, Doc, . . . and everyone else on
> that bucket—all the guys everywhere who sail from
> Tedium to Apathy and back again—with an occasional
> side trip to Monotony . . . I've discovered, Doc, that the
> most terrible enemy of this war is the boredom that
> eventually becomes a faith and, therefore, a sort of sui-
> cide—and I know that the ones who refuse to surrender to
> it must be very strong.[13]

But a telegram arrives informing us that Roberts was
killed in combat just shortly thereafter. Sherwood, Heggen, and Logan have saved their hero from ever having to
return to the boredom of noncombative labor.

Although generally, and probably correctly, admired
for its lampooning of navy life, *Mr. Roberts* can be viewed
as a parable of modern working life as well. Ensign Roberts's frustration at his detachment from combat, that is,
the end-product of his military profession, parallels the
anxiety that overcame workers in large industries and offices as they became further and further removed from the
ultimate purpose of their labor. As Rodgers observes in
The Work Ethic in Industrial America, 1850–1920, the

division of most labor into small meaningless tasks eventually "drove a wedge between art and work, creativity and labor, self and job."[14] The existential dilemmas and crises of identity that occur as a result of the alienation of workers from their work—dilemmas that were hinted at in Barry's *Holiday* and rather broadly abstracted in *The Adding Machine* and *The Hairy Ape*—are quite clearly drawn in this play. While the conscious working out of the meaning of life in terms of work occurs in many postwar dramas, most notably *Death of a Salesman* and *The Glass Menagerie*, it is interesting to observe how full a treatment that problem receives in what is, at base, a romping farce about military idiocy.

Although it is not always a central theme, the theme of combat as an escape from dull work appears in other war dramas. In Elmer Rice's *Flight to the West* (1941), an airborne, wartime "Grand Hotel," we meet law student Charles Nathan who wants to rush out of law school and become an army pilot:

> I've been playing with the idea of being an army pilot. ... I don't know why. It is completely irrational. I certainly have no appetite for fighting in a war or even learning to fight. But I feel I should be doing something more relevant than settling down to the practice of law[15]

Sherwood also exploits this theme in his *There Shall Be No Night* (1940), one of the many American plays to sing the praises of European struggle against the Nazis. In this play we meet two Englishmen who were rejected from the British army for being too old (thirty-six). However, when they heard that Finland was desperate for men in its defense against a Nazi invasion, the two men rushed to that country to join the resistance. Oddly enough, their explanation of their actions downplays their desire to right a wrong and instead emphasizes their need to escape the boredom of their work as furniture salesmen at Harrod's.[16]

The theme of wartime heroics as an escape from the dullness of normal work represents a significant change in the attitudes toward work that were expressed during the depression dramas only a few years earlier. Gone is the pressing need to give a man a job. Gone as well are the sad tales of men and their families struggling against the hardships of poverty. Most significantly, gone is the notion that the battle between a man and his job is a battle of economic and social class. In these newer dramas, it is the boredom and frustration of a single "everyman" and not the dialectic of a class struggle that gives rise to heroism.

The universal dimension of the working man's dilemma during the war is evident in the variety of jobs in which it is manifested. *The Rugged Path, Mr. Roberts,* and the several other dramas that portray war as a grand escape from everyday life play the heroics of war against the meaninglessness of such work as journalism, sales, noncombatant military duty, even the law. In each case, of course, the boring and purposeless life of the working man is fulfilled by the opportunity to fight in a war; the conflict is everywhere and the need for manpower is great. As long as the war is in progress, the artist can hold out to us the hope of escaping one's petty, meaningless job and achieving a larger-than-life heroism. But what happens to the working man when the war is finally over? Conceivably, Morey Vinion would have been forced to live out his life as an insecure editor, Doug Roberts as a benumbed supply officer, and David Nathan as an "irrelevant" attorney. There would be precious little hope for over-aged furniture salesmen at Harrod's as well.

What emerges from these plays is our first glimmering of the postwar, middle-class identity crisis that was to reach its fruition in the works of Miller, Williams, Albee, and others. For if we are to assume from many of these war playwrights that normal, middle-class work is insufficient to fulfill a man's sense of purpose, then it appears that the postwar American faces a terrible conflict. Believing as he does in the moral and economic necessity of daily work, the war will have taught him that it is possible to transcend that normal work and achieve glory along with his material gains. But without the war that knowledge may destroy him. The war saved Doug Roberts and Morey Vinion from dying without fulfilling themselves. But the question remains as to what will happen in peacetime to the likes of Willy Loman.

In addition to exploring the stark, significant contrasts that the world of work and the world of war present to one another, playwrights also found some minor but interesting thematic interplays between the two. Many plays exploited the ironies imbedded in the contrast between the measure of success that soldiers had achieved in the army and their success in the civilian work they left behind them. Much is made of this ironic counterpoint in Harry Brown's *A Sound of Hunting* (1945), a drama about a small troop of American GI's pinned down interminably by an Axis outpost in a small town in Italy. The absurdity of fighting a war by waiting is underscored by the ridiculous comparisons they draw between their roles in the army hierarchy and their roles in civilian life. For example, they often mention the fact that the troop's captain was a college roommate of one of the buck sergeants. But while most of the soldiers feel that the disparity between the two men's ranks is "yet another" example of army injustice, one wise corporal notes that the irony of their different levels of success contains yet another irony within itself.

> [Sergeant] Carter is better off. He's got no responsibility. All he's got to worry about is [his corporal] Collucci. The captain's got a hundred Collucci's to worry about.[17]

Later in the same play the men are called upon to save the life of the troop "screw-up," who has bungled into enemy hands while standing guard duty. The other members of the troop, as well as the readers of the play, are made fully aware of the irony that the soldier who could never do anything right is the most successful man among them back in the states, where he owns a prosperous insurance business.[18] For Brown, the absurdity of war stems not only from the bloodshed of the battle but also from the fact that military life is so alien to the logic and order of the business world that the military pretends to imitate.

Nonetheless, patriotic plays, such as those of Sherwood and Hart, manage to turn the incongruity of a man's military success and his civilian success into a patriotic symbol of the nation's unity in the great cause. For these playwrights the war is the great job that binds all men regardless of their station in civilian life. In Sherwood's *There Shall Be No Night*, Dr. Kaarlo Volken resists the urgings of an American journalist to ignore the war and continue with his ground-breaking studies in social psychology. Instead, the doctor goes into the field of battle and tends the wounded Finnish soldiers and civilians who are combatting the invading Nazis: "There is only one form of work that matters now—resistance, blind dogged desperate resistance." [19]

The wide-eyed air corpsmen in *Winged Victory* come to see their common role of army air pilot as sensible, even if they did hold down a variety of jobs in civilian life:

> Allen. It's kind of funny. I work in a bank, Pinky's a barber, Frankie's a chemist—
> Pinky. Say, where do you think pilots come from? Warner Brothers? They're just like me. [20]

Whereas the difference between a man's civilian and military success bewilders and amuses Laurents and Brown, it exhilarates Sherwood and Hart. For them the war brings together men who are isolated from one another in their pursuit of civilian work, as if somehow the variety of civilian jobs in America symbolized a country out of touch with its sense of national unity. The quasi-Maoist vision they create of the doctor and the ditchdigger standing shoulder to shoulder piling on the sandbags is intended to stir the blood and rally the troops. To the anti-military skeptic, on the other hand, it is merely a reminder that the army does not know the difference between a doctor and a ditchdigger.

Although World War II did not succeed in eliminating all strikes, all labor disputes, all poverty, all unemployment, all farm failures, and all mortgage foreclosures from American life, it certainly succeeded in obliterating them from the American stage. Hardly any character in an American war drama worried about economics. The war had either made his life so desperate that he did not think about his economic well-being or it had invited him to adopt an heroic self-image that permitted him to transcend concern about the basic economic necessities of life. Whether Americans were in uniform or back home, the war as it was presented in American dramas managed to feed and clothe everybody.

This on-stage prosperity carried over into American drama of the postwar period, which reflected the postwar economic boom. The millions of men returning home created a housing boom. Within their booming houses, they supported booming families, and took jobs in booming numbers. With the notable exception of black playwrights of the 1950s and 1960s, who will be discussed in Chapter VI, the American playwright saw the postwar American as a man at work. His job had become a literary donnée.

But the American playwright also saw the postwar working man as a victim of the law of rising expectations. Unlike his counterpart in the 1930s, who needed "something to do" just to have a measure of dignity in his life, the postwar working man required a life that was meaningful as well. The war had taught him that an American working man could be a hero in addition to a jobholder. But what the war did not teach him was how to cope with that need for heroic action and elevated purpose during peacetime. Moreover, it failed to teach him the dangers of conducting a quest for a meaningful, distinctive life in a society that fed on bureaucratic monotony and glad-handing personality manipulation. That lesson was to come a few years later, from Arthur Miller and Tennessee Williams.

V

DEATH OF A SALESMAN, ALL MY SONS, AND THE GLASS MENAGERIE

Arthur Miller's *Death of a Salesman* (1949) and Tennessee Williams's *The Glass Menagerie* (1945) have come to be acknowledged as two of the finest and most important plays of twentieth-century American drama. The frequency with which the plays are revived, reprinted, and anthologized stands as testimony to their firm hold on the attention of American play-reading and play-going audiences. Moreover they are among the few American dramas to receive favorable critical comparison with works by major European playwrights.

Among the many stylistic and thematic innovations that these two plays bring to modern American drama is the view that what are considered social problems in America are also matters of intense crisis for the human spirit. Over and above their astute commentary on American social and economic forces, we find in these plays an examination of the psychological and emotional impact of these forces upon the individual. In each play an individual struggles to find the meaning of his existence, and in each play that struggle is waged against an indifferent or hostile society. To the extent that what John Gassner has called "a sense of tragedy" links the tragic characters of one age to the tragic characters of another, these plays are perhaps the first to connect the American stage and American society to the tradition of dramatic literature that concerns itself with the all-consuming crisis of individuals who try to exert their will upon an unwilling social order.

In *Death of a Salesman* and *The Glass Menagerie*, the

theme of work in modern society is a major concern. In both dramas we find men struggling against unbearable pressures brought upon them by work. But unlike the left-wing protest dramas of the 1930s, these two plays go far beyond the political and economic dimensions of work, although they portray those dimensions thoroughly. Unlike many of the plays of World War II heroism, these works go beyond the individual's need to lead a heroic life in a dull and mundane world, although they reveal that need in their major characters. What separates these two plays from their predecessors is the fact that in each play pressures of work are portrayed as eroding basic elements of human survival and thus threatening man's spiritual and physical existence.

The subject of destructive contemporary attitudes toward work demands that we include for discussion here Arthur Miller's *All My Sons* (1947). Although a lesser work than either *Salesman* or *Menagerie*, it is important to the development of the theme of work in American drama. As do *Salesman* and *Menagerie*, *All My Sons* depicts a man brought to a crisis in his life by his adherence, willful or otherwise, to a philosophy of work that threatens both his physical and his spiritual existence. In *All My Sons*, Joe Keller's attitudes toward his work and his society attack his morals and even his capacity for morality. In *Death of a Salesman*, Willy's attitudes toward his work undermine his capacity for self-knowledge. In *The Glass Menagerie*, Tom Wingfield is compelled by his dependent mother to take a job that threatens his spontaneity and his passion.

Although all three plays are important both to the development of the theme of work in modern American drama and to modern American drama as a whole, it would be misleading to suggest that the three plays are of equal or even nearly equal importance. I find myself in sympathy with those who would call *Death of a Salesman* the most important of the three dramas, if not one of the most important American dramas ever written. It is, as

Tynan has called it, "a triumph of the plain style," although critics frequently take it to be "plainer" than it is. The play has a devastating emotional impact both in performance and in reading. Moreover, it offers perhaps the most complicated and difficult view of American society, and American working life in particular, of any play ever written. Therefore, taking some small liberties with chronology, we shall examine *Death of a Salesman* and *All My Sons* prior to looking at Miller's other relevant works or at the appropriate works of Tennessee Williams.

Thirty-three years after the play's triumphant opening in New York, *Death of a Salesman* now carries with it a considerable amount of critical and scholarly baggage. There have been examinations of such important issues as whether or not it is possible to write a tragedy in modern America, whether or not the Freudian overtones of the Boston scene clash with the play's implied social criticism, whether or not the play's anticapitalist sympathies drain the play of all other merits and purposes, and so on. The difficulty in some of these questions becomes quite apparent when one reads some of the author's contradictory observations on the play. Miller has said that Willy Loman is a common man but has denied that he is average. In one interview he has said that Willy's problems are caused by the fact that he has a fixed set of values, and in the same interview he implied that Willy has no values whatsoever.[1]

There is no question that the play is ambiguous, particularly regarding the relationship of Willy to the modern working world. But the ambiguities, if not entirely intentional, are certainly essential to the portrayal of a working American man (who is both common and average) facing a crisis at the end of a life of hard, exhausting work and unfulfilled fantasies. In order to explore the spiritual aspects of this crisis—such as the recognition of one's own false values, the regret and self-hatred caused by past errors, and the uncontrollable urge to deceive oneself—Miller has had to create a character who is not a realistic, photographic representation of a salesman but an abstraction. For all the name-brand detail that abounds in the play including the Frigidaire, Ebbets Field, the Chevy, and whipped cheese, many central parts of Willy's life, work, and character are only vaguely shaded in.

To begin with, we never learn what product or line of products Willy sells. Miller's decision to keep this information from us is a vital one that is often dismissed too easily when it is not overlooked entirely. If Willy were an entirely "realistic" salesman he would talk endlessly about his product; he would love it, revile it, blame his failures on it, and have fourteen hundred gross of it, whatever it is, lying around the house. But this omission of a specific product permits us to see Willy as a metaphor for all salesmen, if not for all imagemaking in society.

Moreover, the absence of the product points to the evolution of what Riesman has called the other-directed or outer-directed personality in modern society, a vision that Miller shares to a large degree. The outer-directed individual, more a product of his peer group than of his family or of a firm system of internalized values, makes being liked his chief source of direction and chief area of sensitivity. His malaise, says Riesman, stems from the fact that he "is often torn between the illusion that life should be easy if he could only find his way to the proper group-adjustment practices and the half-buried feeling that it is not easy for him."[2] In a society made up of such individuals, the chief economic activity becomes consumption; sales, imagemaking, marketing, and promotion all take priority over production in a society where success is measured not in the ability to produce or even to promote a product but to promote for promotion's own sake.[3] Thus, Willy sells himself, his smile, his appearance, his shoeshine, and ultimately his soul. Like the faltering products in his home that he has purchased from other salesmen and consumed throughout his life, he is wearing out from overuse and is beyond repair. By merging the man and his work so completely, Miller has made work an issue that is humane and human as well as economic and political.

Furthermore, the merging of Willy's being and his work allows Miller to approach work as an abstraction itself: the center of a series of values that holds, or fails to hold, Willy's family together. In the Loman family, love, sex, religion, and all other conventional familial bonds have been superseded or eliminated by the several half-truths and false beliefs that make up the family's philosophy of work. Work here has taken over all spiritual dimensions of life. Thus Willy's work is abstracted so that a life-and-death crisis can emerge from his failed quest for a quasi-religious comfort in his working life and "working faith."

Willy's family background is also abstracted. His relationship to his brother Ben is half memory and half fantasy. Moreover, Ben is the source of the legend of Willy's father, a self-made, nineteenth-century peddler "who made more in a week than [Willy] could make in a lifetime." The abstraction of two pioneer father figures allows Miller to play off Willy's dilemma in modern, rationalized society against the romantic, pioneering spirit that Willy longs for but can never capture. As Barry Edward Gross has pointed out, the pioneering spirit that lives in Willy, Happy, and Biff collides with the demands of work in the modern world and turns all of them into angered, frustrated men.[4] The vague characterizations of Ben and Willy's father permit us to see that Willy's dreams of fulfillment through his work are a full century and a full continent off the mark.

By abstracting the concept of work as it is practiced by both the modern salesman and the romantic pioneer adventurer, Miller makes it possible to write a "social drama" that is quite different from the issue-oriented, predominantly left wing social drama with which the term had been associated previously. Rather than espousing an ideology or trying to change the reader's mind, Miller creates a study of an individual who is entirely at odds with the unwritten philosophies and laws of behavior that his society has established for itself. In his essay "On

Social Plays," Miller cites as his source for social drama the ancient Greek preoccupations with "ultimate law," the "Grand Design," and the "basic assumptions" that a people adopt for guiding their lives. When man, a social being, prospers then he is "engaged" to those laws and assumptions. It is important to note that Miller sees this engagement as being a spiritual or religious condition as well as a political one:

> The individual was at one with his society; his conflicts with it were, in our terms, like family conflicts the opposing sides of which nevertheless shared a mutuality of feeling and responsibility. Thus the drama written for them, while for us it appears wholly religious, was religious for them in more than a mystical way. Religion is the only way we have any more of expressing our genuinely social feelings and concerns, for in our bones we as a people do not otherwise believe in our oneness with a larger group.[5]

Willy Loman is not at one with his society. His basic assumptions, indeed, his Grand Design, are not those of the larger group. Thus his is a spiritual crisis, because for Miller a man who is at odds with society and its basic assumptions is a man "doomed to frustration." And certainly Willy is frustrated by the unresolvable paradox of his attempt to live a life that is fundamentally incorrect for his society. Of course, Willy's failure lies in his misunderstanding of his society's basic assumptions about work: what it means, how one succeeds at it, and how one prepares oneself and one's sons to accept it. As we meet Willy on the last two days of his life, he reveals to us the mistaken assumptions that he has harbored about working life in modern America.

Willy's primary mistake in work and ultimately in his life is the belief that success in work is contingent entirely upon appearances. For example, his faith in his sons' physical attributes is so deep that it even has undertones of master-race psychology:

Bernard can get the best marks in school, y'understand, but when he gets out in the business world, y'understand, you are going to be five times ahead of him. That's why I thank God almighty you're both built like Adonises. Because the man who makes an appearance in the business world is the man who gets ahead.[6]

Not surprisingly, the few psychological rewards that Willy has reaped from his work and effort have been found in his occasional making of successful if deceptive appearances. At various times in the play Willy recalls one of the "great times" in his life when the boys were young. One afternoon he and Biff simonized their old car. The car had such a lovely appearance that the dealer to whom they were selling the car refused to believe there were eighty thousand miles on it. It is this fleeting triumph of appearance, a momentary reinforcement of an almost universally incorrect assumption about work and success, that Willy last remembers before deciding to kill himself on Biff's behalf.

Willy's obsession with appearance leads to a second false assumption about work, namely that he could be more successful at something he appeared to be good at (selling) than something at which he had considerable talent. During the play we learn about Willy's adeptness at carpentry and construction. His successful neighbor, Charley, is impressed with these skills while justifiably unimpressed with almost every other dimension of Willy's life. Willy knows that he is good with his hands and even acknowledges that this skill gives him an aspect of superiority. (At one point he snaps at Charley, "Any man who can't handle tools is not a man.") But Willy is so taken with his work fantasies—the camaraderie of the salesmen, the receptionists, and the mayors, and the giant funeral at the end of the road—that he never recognizes that he has the potential to work successfully and well as a carpenter, producing competent work without any of the glamour and romance attached to selling.[7]

Willy's third mistaken assumption about the nature of work in modern society concerns his belief that by using a "system" or an "angle," a man can circumvent hard work and still gain success. He believes that Biff's popularity can excuse him from studying for his exams. He fantasizes that by fast-talking the receptionists he can be ushered through to the buyers without competing against the other sales-men. He periodically invokes the image of his brother Ben, from whom he hopes to discern the mystery of quick riches for himself and his sons:

> Ben. William, when I walked into the jungle I was seven-teen. When I walked out I was twenty-one. And By God I was rich.
> Willy. . . . was rich! That's the spirit I want to imbue them with. To walk into a jungle. I was right! I was right! I was right![8]

This exchange leads him to conclude, "A man can end with diamonds on the basis of being liked."

Despite these approaches, Willy is not a lazy man. He has worked extremely hard during his forty years with the company. His entire life can be measured by the cadence of his comings and goings from road trips, from which he has never appeared to have a break. But he has aban-doned his faith in hard work for the same reasons that have caused many Americans to do the same; work has ex-hausted him without rewarding him.[9] The society around him promotes hard work that has not resulted in the psy-chological or material benefits that it ought to have provided. Willy's reaction to the unsatisfactory results of his effort appears as fantasies of making it by concocting various impossible Loman Brothers schemes. This reac-tion is Willy's half-conscious act of social revolt and simul-taneous psychological escape. Society's belief in hard work is killing him and he knows it; the fantasy of success without work is part opiate and part rejection of social values. As Harold Clurman notes, one of Willy's more appealing features is that he dies without ever accepting modern society's work values.[10]

But Clurman, among others, is incorrect when he asserts that Miller is directly attacking modern industrialism or the American capitalist system. Miller is portraying a conflict between a society with a particular set of beliefs and a man who, largely through his own very human shortcomings, is unable to live up to that society's expectations of him. In this conflict Miller was not interpreting society as evil, immoral, or even amoral. The society in which Willy Loman lives is based upon a very clear set of beliefs in work that Miller treats not only as nonoppressive but perhaps even necessary if modern men are to live together.

The aspect of this play that is so often neglected by critics, particularly those critics who attribute to it tough-minded, left-wing social criticism, is that Miller's society is not unfathomable to all men. It has certain clear, familiar, traditional values about work and life that are perfectly accessible to common men. These values are embraced by the characters Charley and Bernard, who in their inner peace, their harmony with their society, their material success, and their compassion make a strong case for the persistence of pre-industrial, nineteenth-century work values in modern bourgeois working life.

No one in the play understands Willy better than Charley. He does not have Linda's insight into Willy's relationships with his sons or into his psychological self-destructiveness, but Charley knows all of society's unwritten laws about how a man must conduct his working life, and he knows when those laws are being violated. Thus his comments to and about Willy and his working life represent the play's most insightful comments on Willy's conflict with society.

Even in his memories and fantasies of Biff's halcyon days on the football field, Willy cannot blot out the chiding of the irrepressible Charley, who is the voice of maturity, accommodation, reason, and common sense:

Charley. Knock a homer, Biff, knock a homer!
Willy. I don't think that was funny Charley. This is the greatest day of his life.

Charley. Willy, when are you going to grow up?
Willy. Yeah, heh? When this game is over, Charley, you'll be laughing out of the other side of your face. They'll be calling him another Red Grange. Twenty-five thousand a year.
Charley. *kidding* Is that so . . . Well, then, I'm sorry. But tell me something . . . Who is Red Grange?[11]

Charley's confidence in the imminent failure of Willy's dreams does not stem from any prior knowledge about the particulars of the day: he has no reservations about Biff's football abilities, and he has no prior knowledge of Biff's future difficulties with the math regents exam. Charley simply knows that the unwritten societal laws regarding working hard, applying oneself, and not trying to get rich quick are being violated and that in some way society will exact its punishment. Charley also knows that trying to explain all this to Willy is futile, since his attempt to do so during Ben's visit a few years earlier had been disastrous.

In that scene, during which Willy shows off to Ben by touting his sons' fearlessness, Charley tries to balance the temptation that Ben's life of adventure offers to Willy with his own example of honesty, moderate behavior, integrity, self-discipline, and security. As Charley enters, we learn that Biff has been stealing materials from a nearby construction site:

Charley. Listen, if they steal any more from that building, the watchman'll put the cops on them!
Linda *to Willy.* Don't let Biff . . . *Ben laughs lustily* . . .
Willy. I got a couple of fearless characters there.
Charley. Willy, the jails are full of fearless characters.
Ben. *clapping Willy on the back with a laugh at Charley.* And the stock exchange, friend.[12]

While Charley and Ben do not directly represent a moral good and a moral evil, they are the polar opposites of Willy's dilemma: the hard, compromising way to harmony with one's society or the bold, antiwork fantasy of fast

riches. This scene is perhaps too simply structured for
Miller's purposes, but it does underscore the fact that
Charley's world is cogent, moral, sound, possible, and, in
comparison to Ben's brutality, even humane.

The most telling of Charley's insights into Willy's
conflict with society, and the clearest indication that he
has understood Willy in ways Linda never could, comes in
the requiem scene at Willy's funeral. Here Linda reveals
that, although she understood Willy as a man, she no more
understood the world of work and the pressures it exacted
on him than Willy himself did. In addition to expressing
her grief, she indicates that she is puzzled over why Willy
would kill himself. The house was paid for, he was finished
at the dentist, and they were "free and clear." The suicide
amazes her because "He only needed a little salary." More
telling even than his "Willy was a salesman" eulogy is
Charley's response: "No man only needs a little salary."
Charley knows that a man needs to accept the values of his
society, not simply out of conversion or obligation but out
of a sense of harmony and permanence about himself and
his society. Charley also knows that Willy needed to
recognize that the system he sought to beat was the very
heart of his society, which was as vital to him as it was to
any other man. Moreover, Charley understands that in
Willy's final error of judgment, namely that a working
man is worth more dead than alive, Willy had attempted
unsuccessfully to bring himself into harmony with his son
and his society by giving his son a "gilt-edged" $20,000
insurance payoff and showing him an enormous salesman's
funeral. Of course Willy failed.

The fact that Charley's values regarding work truly
are clear and consistent laws of society and not just the
fortuitous triumph of a single man is made clear to us in
the success of Bernard. Just as Willy has bequeathed to
his sons the confusion and self-destruction of his own incorrect assessment of work in society, Charley has passed
on to Bernard the correct social values of hard work and
careful self-evaluation that guarantee the very success that

Willy sought. At seventeen, Bernard knows more about the world of work than Willy ever learns:

> Biff, I heard Mr. Birnbaum say that if you don't start studyin' math, he's gonna flunk you and you won't graduate. . . . Just because he printed University of Virginia on his sneakers doesn't mean they've got to graduate him, Uncle Willy.[13]

Bernard also shares his father's feeling of charity toward the weaker Loman men. Like Charley, who helps Willy by giving him "loans" and perpetually offering him a safe job, Bernard merely ignores the Lomans' insults about his bookishness and freely gives of himself to help Biff with math. But even as a young man Bernard knows the rules; he knows who he is and where he is going. When Willy asks him to jeopardize himself on behalf of Biff, the boy refuses without a moment's hesitation:

> Bernard. Where is he? If he doesn't study!
> Willy. *You'll give him the answers.*
> Bernard. I do, but I can't on the Regents exam. They're liable to arrest me.[14]

The unwavering correctness of young Bernard's values is borne out in the scene in Charley's office in which Willy confronts the adult Bernard on his way to argue a case in front of the Supreme Court. Now fully aware that Bernard knows "the secret" of success, Willy humbles himself to ask Bernard how "it is done." It should be noted, of course, that while Willy is desperate to know the answer, he cannot bring himself to accept fully Bernard's pronouncements of society's unwritten laws for success and fulfillment at work:

> Bernard. You know, "if at first you don't succeed."
> Willy. Yes, I believe in that.
> Bernard. But sometimes, Willy, it's better for a man to just walk away.
> Willy. Walk away?
> Bernard. That's right.

Willy. But if you can't walk away?
Bernard. *after a slight pause.* I guess that's when it's
tough.[15]

As Miller indicates in a later essay, "On Social Plays,"
Willy's failure lies in his inability to fit the "pattern of efficiency" in American working life. But Miller does not
suggest that the pattern of efficiency is evil or cruel or
should be overthrown. He does say that it is deficient in
that it is not accompanied by a standard of behavior or a
means of generating respect for the individual that is in
any way removed from the function of doing work. While
this attitude is lamentable and Miller laments it, his
dramas offer analysis, not manifesto. He recognizes that
the demise of the world's Willy Lomans is caused by their
inability to accommodate themselves to "a scheme of
things that is not at all ancient but very new in the
world."[16] Moreover, society does not make such an adjustment easy for Willy; there are temptations to be resisted
and mistakes to be avoided. But Willy is still free to fall
and to fail. His is not a tragedy of the evils of capitalism
but instead a tragedy of failed social adjustment—a new
but devastating sea of troubles against which modern men
occasionally take arms.[17]

Salesman is important to the development of the
work theme in American drama, not only because it influences later dramas but also because it expands the scope
of American drama to include the humanistic implications
of modern work that were explored in Elmer Rice's *The
Adding Machine* in 1923. Both Rice and Miller felt that
the best way to approach humanistically the problems of
modern work was to portray an Everyman engaged in a
hopeless battle against modern industrialism. Granted,
Rice's flat, unappealing Mr. Zero and Miller's moving
Willy Loman are not created to serve the same dramatic
purposes, but it is important to note that they are both
fighters and losers in a life-and-death struggle in the world
of modern work (a "zero" and a "low man"). Like Zero's,

Willy's life crisis culminates in his sudden dismissal after a lifetime of work doing the same thing for the same company. Like Zero's, Willy's home life is a reflection of the problems that confront him at work. Both Zero and Willy are also unequal to the task of resolving their domestic difficulties. But most importantly, both Zero and Willy have become so exhausted by their life of work that they have lost the ability to reach peace with themselves or even to save themselves when the opportunity to do so is presented to them.

Zero and Willy both arrive at the end of their respective plays with a defeated spirit. Zero, already dead and reliving his mistakes in the afterlife, is incapable of understanding the causes of his misery. Offered another chance for life on earth, he eagerly runs back to the same adding machine and the same numbing, white-collar bureaucracy that degraded his spirit in his first life. Willy ends with a last-ditch, misguided effort to win the love of his son and to "set him up" financially through a twenty-thousand-dollar insurance payoff (which the company, ultimately, refuses to pay). He is so bewildered about who he is and so confused by the world in which he has worked for forty years that he is incapable of accepting his son's love without offering in return a twenty-thousand-dollar gift.

But of these examinations of two crushed souls, certainly Miller's is the more thoughtful and the more forgiving. While the message of *The Adding Machine* is one of nihilism and unmitigated disdain for both the modern man and the modern age, the effect of *Death of a Salesman* is complex and ambiguous. The failure of the marriage of Willy Loman's values to the unwritten laws of his society is one that levels comparable blame on both the man and the society. Both the man and his society have needs that are genuine, but neither can meet the needs of the other.

Ultimately, of course, the pathos in *Salesman* stems from Willy and not society because Willy is human, Willy has a spiritual dimension to his being, and Willy will lose in his conflict with his society. Unlike Zero, who ultimately becomes as despicable as the society that ruins him, Willy ends as a being apart from his society. He dies a frustrated man in a last vain effort to reconcile the ill-fated union of his values with those of society. It is Willy's immense effort at this reconciliation that is moving and even heroic. Prior to Miller's play, no American playwright had ever successfully blended the world of work with the multifaceted dimensions of the human psyche and the most searching questions of human existence. Thus, *Death of a Salesman* brings the theme of work to its highest point in the American drama.

In his earlier play *All My Sons* (1947), Miller had already begun to evolve a view of working life as consuming the entirety of human experience. In his character of Joe Keller, the munitions manufacturer who knowingly sends faulty airplane cylinders to the army in order to avoid delaying the order, Miller created a man who is physically, intellectually, and emotionally carved out of his work. Not a subhuman anthropoid like Yank in *The Hairy Ape*, Joe Keller is merely a man who is as complex, as hardworking, as dedicated, and as amoral as the industrialized century that produced him:

> a heavy man of stolid mind and build, a businessman these many years, but with the imprint of the machine-shop worker and boss still upon him. When he reads, when he speaks, when he listens, it is with the terrible concentration of the uneducated man for whom there is still wonder in many commonly known things, a man whose judgment must be dredged out of experience and a peasant-like common sense.[18]

And so, much like Willy, Joe Keller interprets his world through the demands of his work. His dream is that his living son, Chris, will take over the factory. He hopes for reconciliation with his former partner, who took all the blame for the faulty cylinder heads, by giving him a job when he gets out of jail. He reads the want ads of the newspaper to see "how people make a living—to see what they want."

When it is revealed that Keller is responsible for the sending of the cylinder heads and the subsequent death of twenty young pilots, Keller offers a defense of his actions that is passionate, sympathetic, and almost convincing because he does indeed have something meaningful to defend—his entire life's work:

> I'm in business, a man is in business; one hundred and twenty cracked, you're out of business. You got a process, the process don't work, you're out of business; you don't know how to operate, your stuff is no good; they close you up, they tear up your contracts, what the hell's it to them? You lay forty years into a business, and they knock you out in five minutes. What could I do, let them take forty years, let them take my life away?[19]

Moreover, Keller quite correctly sees himself as part of a larger system of work and profit, a system that operates under society's sanctions and a system whose rules he did not break. As far as Keller is concerned, he is as much a victim of the demands of this system as anyone else:

> Listen, you gotta appreciate what was doin' in that shop in the war. The both of you. It was a madhouse. Every half hour the major calling for cylinder heads, they were whippin' us with the telephone. The trucks were haulin' em away, hot damn near. I mean just try to see it human, see it human.[20]

And he is no more blameful of anything than is anyone else:

> Who worked for nothing in that war? When they work for nothing, I'll work for nothing. Did they ship a gun or a truck out of Detroit before they got their price. Is that clean? It's dollars and cents, nickels and dimes; war and peace, it's nickels and dimes. Half the goddam country's gotta go if I go.[21]

But as passionate, sympathetic, and desperate as his explanations are, Keller is still held responsible for his actions by his son Chris, an officer during World War II who speaks for Miller at the end of the play:

> Where do you live? Where have you come from? I was dying every day you were killing my boys and you did it for me? What the hell do you think I was thinking of, the Goddam business? Is that as far as your mind can see, the business? What is that—the world? The business. What the hell do you mean you did it for me? Don't you have a country? Don't you live in the world?[22]

Despite the harshness of the attack that Miller levels against Joe Keller's defense of his actions, Miller is less concerned with taking immoral capitalists to task than he is with examining the absence of morality in society. Although Joe's is a clear case of war profiteering, we learn quickly that he is not motivated by greed, lust for power, antiworker prejudice, or any of the other stock evils of Marxist protest literature. Joe's problem is that work and success have cost him his moral vision. He kills twenty men, he destroys his partner's family, and eventually he kills himself. What troubles Miller is that Joe has so completely woven the fabric of his life into his work that he is incapable of interpreting anything in the world that lies outside of it. For Miller the most important dimension of human existence that lies, or at least that should lie, outside of the demands of work is morality: "a standard of values that will create in man a respect for himself." The fact that Keller, like many other businessmen, is reacting to real pressures of industrial America ("half the country's gotta go" if he goes), does not vindicate Keller but implicates the entire society for its failure to provide a standard of morality independent of the standards of work and success that rule the existences of men like Joe Keller or Willy Loman.

All My Sons and *Death of a Salesman* explore two facets of the American working man that Miller discusses in "On Social Plays." The former play explores the failure of men to create a standard of morality that is not subservient to the pattern of efficiency that dominates modern industrial society. The latter play explores the tensions between the "unwritten laws" of societal behavior and the individual who must either adapt himself to those laws or suffer a life of endless frustration. But in both plays, Miller openly acknowledges that in modern America the work place is where the individual makes peace or war with his society. Society will ultimately judge his behavior on the job, whether that judgment is rendered on a strictly profit-oriented basis or from an independent standard of morality that stands in open defiance of that profit motive.

We should observe that the idea of the American individual carving out his identity from his work is a major theme in two other plays by Miller. In *A View from the Bridge* (1955), Italian immigrants struggle to find work on the docks of New York while eluding the immigration authorities. Not only a means of earning a living, a job in New York becomes the core of "Americanness" for the quintessential American in the early twentieth century—the immigrant. In *The Price* (1968) two brothers, a policeman and a surgeon, discover that their choices of career have been guided by their deepest feelings of guilt and responsibility toward their father and toward each other. In this play, adult careers become the outward manifestation of basic emotional needs left unfulfilled in childhood.

Miller appears to be saying, then, that in modern America it is the relationship between a man and his work that provides perhaps the richest possible source for great drama, for it is in the work place that the crises of great drama are acted out. The work place is where man struggles for physical survival. The work place is where he confronts the elements that threaten his sense of himself. The work place is where he declares himself to be of value to his society, and it is at work that society chooses to recognize that value or not. If he succeeds in fulfilling society's unwritten laws of profit motive and success, he will do so at work. If he succeeds in finding a human center to his life, a set of values by which he may retain his humanity, he will have to do so in defiance of his work. If we can accept Miller's premise that work in America tests a man as thoroughly as did the Greek gods in classical drama, then we can accept his plays of common, working men as the social tragedies they are intended to be.

The emergence of Tennessee Williams at the same time as Arthur Miller has invited comparisons between them. While the differences between their dramatic styles and literary themes have been duly noted by many drama critics, the two playwrights have some similar insights into the state of the modern America, insights that are all the more intriguing because of the very different artists who share them. In his essay "American Blues . . ." Kenneth Tynan notes that Williams's and Miller's early works have shared two "joint ventures": their criticism of the "familiar ogre of commercialism, the killer of values and the leveller of men" and modern man's frustration. "Techniques change, but grand themes do not. Whether in a murder trial, a bullfight, a farce like *Charley's Aunt* or a tragedy like *Lear*, the behavior of a human being at the end of his tether is the common denominator of all drama."[23] What Tynan fails to mention is that these two "joint ventures" can be seen as a shared response, political and visceral, to work in America. For in his play *The Glass Menagerie* Williams presents us with an irresolvable conflict between meaningless, rationalized modern work and the passion and romance that are for Williams the life's blood of men who are intellectually and spiritually alive.

We see an early treatment of this theme in Williams's short play *Moony's Kid Don't Cry* (1940). Moony, a semiarticulate but somehow poetic factory worker, understands completely how modern factory work is grinding up his spirit as well as the souls of his oblivious fellow workers:

> I look at tings diffrunt...Other guys—you know how it is—they don't care. They eat, they drink, they sleep with their women. . . . The sun keeps rising and Saturday night

> they get paid . . . [and] someday they kick off . . . My God, Jane. I want something more than just that.[24]

Irritated by his wife's capitulation to their oppression and meaningless existence ("There *ain't* no more than just that"), Moony lapses into an angry, violent escape fantasy. Invoking the spirit of independence of the pre-industrial age craftsmen who owned their own labor and found meaning in their work, Moony longs to do something significant with his hands:

> [My hands] are so kind of empty and useless . . . I feel like I oughta be doin' something with these two hands of mine besides what I'm doin' now—runnin' bolts through an everlastin' chain.[25]

But since he cannot, he dreams of taking an axe into his hand and of smashing away at the "Smoke, whistles, plants, factories, buildings, buildings buildings" to get to where "it's clear." The fantasy, which ends abruptly when his baby cries in the next room, combines the spirit of the independent pioneer woodsman and the anger of the proletarian revolutionary. However, unlike Tom Wingfield in *Menagerie*, Moony cannot bring himself to act upon his intense desires to escape.

Although the impressionistic technique, the declaration of the drama as a "memory play," and the haunting relationship between Tom and Laura tend to distract attention from the play's social commentary, *The Glass Menagerie* contains as straightforward an attack on the modern system of work and the middle class that succumbs to it as can be found anywhere in postwar American drama:

> I turn back time to that quaint period, the thirties, when the huge middle class of America was matriculating in a school for the blind. Their eyes had failed them or they had failed their eyes, and so they were having their fingers pressed forcibly down on the fiery Braille alphabet of a dissolving economy. In Spain there was revolution. Here there was only shouting and confusion. In Spain there was Guernica. Here there were disturbances of labor.[26]

Yet Williams, like Miller, is far more interested in the toll that such an economic system takes upon the human spirit and the ability to live a life that is meaningful, dignified, and passionate than he is in the "fairness" of one system of economics or another:

> The Wingfield apartment is in the rear of the building, one of those vast hive-like conglomerations of cellular living that flower as warty growths in overcrowded urban centers of lower middle-class population and are symptomatic of the impulse of this largest and fundamentally enslaved section of American society to avoid fluidity and differentiation and to exist and function as one interfused mass of automatism.[27]

Although Tom seems to dismiss the social context of the drama as merely "the social background of the play," Williams does not, as we quickly learn in Tom's confrontations with his mother. To Williams, Amanda represents the dying but not quite dead pre-industrial work values of rural America, both in her inability to understand the emptiness in her own life and in her insistence that Tom surrender his rebellious lust for adventure in the name of conformity to traditional values of self-reliance, self-sacrifice, and hard work:

> Amanda. Most young men find adventures in their careers.
> Tom. Then most young men are not employed in a ware-house.
> Amanda. The world is full of young men employed in warehouses and offices and factories.
> Tom. Do all of them find adventures in their careers?
> Amanda. They do or they do without it. Not everybody has a craze for adventure.
> Tom. Man is by instinct a lover, a hunter, and fighter, and none of these instincts are given much play at the warehouse.
> Amanda. Man is by instinct! Don't quote instinct to me! Instinct is something that people have got away from! It belongs to animals. Christian adults don't want it.[28]

As in *Death of a Salesman*, the world of work represents a threat to the very essence of man. Williams perceives man to be a passionate, instinctive, impulsive being who is denied this crucial dimension of his humanity by being forced to work at something tedious and respectable. The tedium of the warehouse job causes a crisis in Tom's life that is so deep it breaks down his not inconsiderable sense of obligation to his mother and even penetrates his intense love for his sister, Laura.

If Tom is the irrepressible romantic who will not be held by the constraints of an aging society's fading work ethic, Laura is that society's most helpless prisoner. A physical cripple, she is also a societal cripple for she cannot, as her mother so insidiously reminds her, bring herself to cope with the task of learning a job skill:

> Amanda (to Laura). So what are we going to do the rest of our lives. Stay home and watch the parades go by? Amuse ourselves with the glass menagerie, darling? Eternally play those worn out phonographs your father left as a painful reminder of him? We won't have a business career—we've given that up because it gave us indigestion.[29]

Tom is too strong to succumb to society's demands on working, self-sufficient, upwardly mobile young people, but Laura is too weak either to resist or to accept those demands. She cannot work, but she cannot defy the practical necessity of work. She does not escape by fighting but by playing with her fragile glass figurines within the prison of her mother's house. But she is linked to Tom for she too is the child of a man who found no happiness in Amanda Wingfield's joyless house of self-discipline, responsibility, and bourgeois social climbing. And as the last remaining family prisoner of Amanda's empty value system, she is finally called upon by Tom to "blow out the candles," to blot out that time and place from his memory.

It might not have been necessary for Tom to escape from his mother's house and way of life if her values were to die with her. But through Jim, the gentleman caller, we learn that the gods of success, upward mobility, and ambition have been passed to a new generation, fully equipped with the gizmos and gadgets of twentieth-century technology. His faith in shallow appearances and personality manipulation is strikingly similar to Willy Loman's and perfectly compatible with Amanda's:

> Primarily it amounts to—social poise! Being able to square up to people and hold your own on any social level.[30]

But unlike Amanda, whose faith in traditional, rural work values is grounded in a dying past, Jim's faith in work and success is aimed at the future. He explains his philosophy while telling Laura of his visit to the Century of Progress exhibit in Chicago:

> What impressed me most was the Hall of Science. Gives you an idea of what the future will be in America, even more wonderful than the present time.[31]

Because he is the first gentleman caller Laura has ever had, Jim represents a romantic hope to Amanda. But symbolically his values represent the hope for the survival of her own values of hard work, self-sacrifice, and voluntary enslavement to the work system; she sees him as a role model for Tom, a caretaker for Laura, and a savior for herself. But just as his values hold out a false hope for a wonderful America, he holds out a false hope to Amanda Wingfield. Totally mistaken in his assessment of Laura's real needs, tolerant but uncomprehending of Tom's love for adventure, and virtually oblivious to his own problems, Jim is David Riesman's outerdirected man: soulless, and image conscious, he seeks only to talk, to sell, and to "ZZZZZZZp" his way from "the ground floor" to "the top."

This searing social commentary on American working life stops short of being a realistic drama, for memory, magic, and the turning back of time allow for the triumph of Tom Wingfield's poetic soul and restless spirit. In a fit of rage after discovering that Jim is engaged to be married, Amanda tells Tom to "go to the moon." Tom responds with a triumphant, final dash down the fire escape that renders the world of conformity, hard work, and familial responsibility a distant if painful memory:

> I didn't go to the moon. I went much further . . . I descended the steps of this fire-escape for the last time and followed, from then on, in my father's footsteps, attempting to find in motion what was lost in space—I traveled around a great deal. The cities swept about me like dead leaves, leaves that were brightly colored but torn away from the branches. . . . Then all at once my sister touches my shoulder, I turn around and look into her eyes . . . Oh Laura, Laura, I tried to leave you behind me, but I am more faithful than I intended to be.[32]

Although *The Glass Menagerie* is more concerned with a man's memory of his family than it is with his memory of his job, the work from which Tom flees is more than a mere catalyst for his rejection of the past. It is the link between his family and the larger society, both of which trap him and confine him to a world that has stripped itself of its poetry and imagination. Tom's perspective of the values of work upheld by Amanda and Jim is the greatest obstacle to an existence that is meaningful and dignified. Willy Loman and Joe Keller share Tom's view in this respect.

What distinguishes Tom from Willy and Joe is that he is aware of the danger to him that lies in his mother's values and attitudes toward work. Moreover, he is able to substitute an alternative set of values and act upon them. This difference suggests that Williams sees man as free to walk away from his society and its constrictions whereas Miller clearly sees man as a being that cannot survive outside of his society. Unlike Tom, Willy and Joe must come to terms with their working lives, or die trying. This difference further suggests that, at least in this play, Williams condemns his society as hopeless, moribund, and disfunctional. But for Miller there is the hope and belief that society can reform itself; characters like Bernard, Charlie, and Chris Keller hold out for society the hope that social adjustment is possible without the loss of principle, self-worth, or self-knowledge. It is not an easy adjustment, for there will always be men like Joe Keller and Willy Loman, and society itself will continue to invite common and even uncommon men to make mistakes. But Miller believes that both the society and the men who live in it are vital, and thus capable of adjusting to one another. His is the role of the social physician, probing and analyzing the living society in front of him. On the other hand, Williams seems to adopt the role of the anthropologist in *The Glass Menagerie*. He examines from a distance the ruins of Amanda's dead civilization. Psychological probing gives way to a sense of detached curiosity, as if Williams were trying to restore a small measure of life and movement to mummies and skeletons.

It is generally acknowledged that the plays of Miller and Williams had a considerable impact upon young writers of the postwar period, who were moved as much by the "Americanness" of the dramas as by their quality. It is not surprising, then, that we find in the plays of other dramatists of the late 1940s and early 1950s treatments of the theme of work in modern America that use the conflict between the individual and his work as a means of exploring the complexities of the soul and the meaning of modern life. Among the most notable of these is Paddy Chayefsky, whose television play *The Mother* (1954) tells the story of an aging woman who looks back upon her lifetime of scrimping and hard work in an effort to assess its meaning. As the play ends, we see her going out of force of habit from one dead-end seamstress job to another, although it has dawned upon her that the rationale for that lifetime habit never really made sense:

> Oh how we scraped in that store. We used to sell bread for six cents a loaf. I remember my husband saying, "Let's buy a grocery store, at least we'll always have food in the house." It seems to me my whole life was spent hand-to-

mouth . . . I don't know what it all means, I really don't
. . . I'm sixty-six years old and I don't know what the
purpose of it all was.[33]

In his romance *Middle of the Night* (1957), Chayefsky
tells the story of a widower businessman who has come to
see his daily work as a preparation for his retirement and
his retirement as a preparation for his death. To keep himself from facing the absurdity of his existence, he recites
the ritual of his daily routine to assure himself that his life
at least has some structure even if it has no meaning: "I
come home, I want to watch a little TV, I go to sleep. I do
a hard day's work."[34] But Chayefsky rescues him; he falls
in love with a young woman at his factory. While he
regrets that his age and his exhaustion limit his ability to
enjoy the pleasure she has brought him, he mutters at the
end of the play, "Even a few years of happiness you don't
throw away. We'll get married."

Other dramatists, such as Lorraine Hansberry, Edward Albee, Lonne Elder, and even Neil Simon were later
to explore the intense interrelationships between American identity and American working life. But before examining these playwrights and how they advanced the social
insights in Williams's and Miller's work, it is important
to note the thematic connection that Williams and Miller
were able to make with major social drama of the past,
particularly that of Anton Chekhov. Certainly comparisons between Chekhov and Williams have been noted before. The style, tone, and moods of their plays are remarkably similar. They also share an extraordinary ability to
present on the page the most subtle movements of that
almost imperceptible process by which one age becomes
another. They both share the same belief that the conquest
of one generation's values by another's is only superficially
arrived at by great political revolutions and social upheavals. At the core of generations and societies are individuals' slow ascendencies and descendencies, growing
and dying a little each day like so many plants in a garden.
It is not surprising, then, that both men treat the

theme of work very similarly in two of their major works on the subject. In *The Cherry Orchard* and in *The Glass Menagerie*, the revolutionary social upheavals that change their respective society's vision of work are played out in the quiet domestic interplay of characters conducting their normal, ordinary business and conversations with one another. Just as Lopahin's ceremonial purchase of the orchard signals the conquest of the hardworking proletariat over the indolent aristocracy, so does Jim O'Connor's casual announcement that he will not be returning to visit the Wingfields announce the death of the genteel, aristocratic Old South at the hands of the fast-paced industrialist. Despite the fact that Amanda shares with Jim a fundamental belief in hard work and success, her mind and spirit are too tightly bound to the dead days on Blue Mountain. In the eyes of these playwrights, turn-of-the-century Russia and postwar America are so oriented toward the future that all work is geared to the killing off of the past from which the present has so violently seized its power. But somehow the killing is done gently: over dinner, in the parlor, at the train station, in the quietest and gentlest of conversations.

The thematic links between Chekhov and Miller are less obvious because the style and tone of their plays, as well as their balancing of societal and universal concerns, are handled so differently. Miller's stock-in-trade, the critics tell us, is hard-boiled Ibsenism, not poetic textures or probing, still-life portraits of moribund men caught in moribund societies. But in *Death of a Salesman* Miller used precisely the same technique for exploring the spiritual implications of work to individuals as Chekhov did in *The Cherry Orchard*, *The Three Sisters*, and *Ivanov*. Specifically, he abstracted the concept of work. In order to discuss work in its fullest human dimensions he, like Chekhov, made certain that the audience see absolutely no work being done on the stage. Instead all we see of the Lomans is the spiritual, psychological, and material wreckage that a lifetime of work has left behind.

Work and the Work Ethic

As astute observers of two entirely different societies, both men saw two entirely different kinds of work crises. Chekhov saw a generation of people adrift in their own indolence because they did not need to perform productive work; Miller saw a generation of people frustrated because no one existed except to do productive work. But each man sensed that a society whose working life was out of balance with the other dimensions of human life, whether at one extreme or the other, is a society peopled by struggling, purposeless souls. And the impact of the crises faced by people in conflict with their working lives is most profoundly felt in the dramas of both writers because of, not despite, the fact that we never see the professor professing, the schoolteacher teaching, the writer writing, the mail clerk clerking, or the salesman selling. Unlike Hauptmann, Gorki, and the generation of American left-wing naturalists and social realists who protested injustices by showing us suffering working people doing their work, Miller and Chekhov took us into the homes and hearts of working people. They knew that the true strength of a storm is measured most accurately not by the velocity of the winds but by the amount of damage it leaves behind.

It does not strike me as coincidental, then, that the American drama comes of age at precisely the same time and through the very same plays in which the theme of work comes of age in American drama. The maturity of the early Williams and Miller plays lies largely in their effective dramatization of profound universal truths that are embedded in the meaningful particulars of American society. Moreover, these early dramas have taught us that as much as any other aspect of modern American society, work affords an artist a rich opportunity to seek out those truths. A person's work is as particular and individualized as anything he has; yet its bearing upon his identity, his self-image, his dignity, and the meaning of his life is common to almost all people in all societies. Clearly the much-touted technical and artistic maturity of these early plays is accompanied by the artists' mature and sophisticated understanding of modern working life, an understanding that links American social drama to the greatness of Chekhov's social drama and thus elevates the stature of American drama itself.

VI

THE 1960S

By and large, the 1960s did not inspire among dramatists the degree of interest in exploring the intense relationships between people's identities and their jobs that we have seen in previous decades. Although Miller and Williams retained some influence on the drama of this period, playwrights of the 1960s were more profoundly influenced by the rising theater movements that were far more radical, both artistically and politically, than were the comparatively conventional dramas of Miller and Williams. Beckett, Ionesco, and other "absurdist" playwrights of Europe picked up an avid following in America among native playwrights, audiences, actors, and critics. Julian Beck's Living Theater and other "guerrilla" theater troupes rekindled an interest in the theories of Artaud, who held that plays should not be written by authors but should be created by actors and directors through the violent tension of performing on the stage. Many militant black theater artists rejected the idea of writing and producing plays for "white audiences" and created politically oriented community theaters in various cities throughout the country.

These theater movements, which sought to shock middle-class play readers and theater goers, found a strong ally in the political issues of the day, which the middle class found even more shocking than the theater. Black power, the Vietnam War, homosexuals' rights, Indians' rights, drugs, the rebellion of white middle-class youth, and the aura of massive violence that surrounded all of these issues yielded an immense opportunity for theatrical adaptation and exploitation. Not surprisingly, every one of these issues found its way into several dramas of the 1960s.

The sheer massiveness of mass-movement politics seemed to dissipate some of the interest that playwrights and audiences may have had in exploring the souls of little men doing little jobs in a bureaucratic society. Neither the politics nor the theater of the period lent itself to the contemplative, reflective character analyses that typified such domestic works as *Death of a Salesman* or Chayefsky's *Middle of the Night*. Nor did they tend to generate many intensive searches for social values that were far removed from the particular issues and the antirational disposition that seemed to characterize the decade.[1] Thus one finds in the work of Arthur Kopit, Jack Gelber, the early works of Sam Shepard, and in most of the more revolutionary plays of the black theater important social commentary with little attention to the careful working out of the problems of work in the 1960s.[2]

But neither work-related themes nor the enlarged humanistic scope that Miller and Williams brought to them vanished entirely from the scene. In the sixties black playwriting finally received long overdue recognition, largely on the strength of the handling of work themes by such playwrights as Lorraine Hansberry, Lonne Elder III, and Douglas Turner Ward. Themes concerning work and the work ethic are evident in notable early plays by Edward Albee: *The Zoo Story*, *The American Dream*, and particularly *Who's Afraid of Virginia Woolf?* Neil Simon, whose degree of commercial success is rivaled only by the degree to which academic critics revile him, skillfully exploited the relationship between people and their work in several of his comedies of the 1960s. Thus these three areas of discussion—black plays, early works of Albee, and Neil Simon comedies—will form the basis of our examination of work in the drama of that most dramatic decade.

One sees reflected in the work-related themes of black dramas (both during and prior to the 1960s) elements of what historian Eugene Genovese has called the black work ethic (work philosophies and attitudes that grow out of the uniqueness of the black experience in America) as well as values and beliefs that blacks share with other American groups.[3] As Lawrence Levine observes in *Black Culture and Black Consciousness,* nineteenth-century blacks, both free men and slaves, adhered to the agrarian ethic, which held that "the results of labor belong to the laborer." Moreover, Levine observes that, like whites in the nineteenth century, blacks found themselves caught up in and at odds with the rapid change in American society from a rural, decentralized economy to an industrialized economy:

> Emancipation took place in a society rapidly becoming industrialized, urbanized, and centralized, but which in its popular culture, was still mesmerized by the image of the individual as architect of his own destiny.[4]

The fact that many blacks in the late nineteenth century first learned to read from *McGuffy's Reader* and other conservative, inspirational literature of the period helped to re-enforce that image among blacks as well as among whites.[5]

Yet historians like Genovese and Levine assert that the attitudes of blacks toward work were also shaped by their African culture and their slave experiences, a line of inquiry that to this day remains very controversial and very sensitive in the black community—among academics and nonacademics alike. Genovese postulates, for example, that in the nineteenth century blacks did not internalize the time-oriented routines of the industrial system in the mid-nineteenth century because the plantation system heavily re-enforced traditional, rural values. Immigrant Europeans, on the other hand, were whisked right off the boats into industrial centers that gradually transformed them into "suitable" industrial workers.[6] Genovese also sees evidence in the development of Afro-American culture of a preference for work that is done collectively, in which the entire black community would participate, sing, and celebrate while performing an enormous amount of work.[7] And, as many historians have observed, the injustices and the cruelty of the slavery system often gave rise to adversary relationships in slave culture between worker (slave) and employer (overseer or master).[8]

It is this most obvious facet of slave life that doubtless forms Willis Richardson's view of work in his 1923 play, *The Chipwoman's Fortune*. In this drama blacks are victimized by an unjust system of work and economics that is run by whites specifically to benefit themselves at the expense of blacks. With no rewards available to blacks who work, Richardson seeks a way to commend blacks for other virtues. Silas Green is an upright, hardworking porter who supports his family and an unrelated "Aunt Nancy." Silas loses his job when his white boss and a white creditor conspire to "teach him a lesson" (they are incensed that Green has missed a payment on a Victrola he purchased from one of his boss's friends). Silas seems hopelessly caught in a double bind: he cannot return to work if he cannot pay off the debt, and he cannot earn money to pay off the debt if he cannot work. But suddenly Aunt Nancy's wayward son appears and, in gratitude for the kindness Silas has shown to his mother, pays off the debt on the Victrola just as the repossessors show up. The play ends with a happy reunion of mother and son, the family's retention of the record player, and Silas's return to his work. It is important to note that Silas was never rewarded for his labor but was, instead, rewarded for kindness, a compensating virtue. Other early black plays, such as Theodore Ward's *Big White Fog* (1938), offer bitter protests against the life of poverty to which black working people are subjected and thus anticipate some of the acrimony of the plays of the 1960s black protest movement.

However, the conservative, pre-industrial agrarian values that Genovese observes in nineteenth-century black culture are reflected in Ward's later play, *Our Lan'* (1946), a play about the struggle of freedmen to build a life on an island off the Georgia coast. The Puritanism reflected in the black characters is striking, particularly in their grim desire to tame the wilderness by hard work and methodical self-discipline. The group's leader, Joshua, regularly exhorts his people to work hard so that they might "gain the glory":

> Gimme er fiah yonder, 'n er hammer 'n er pair of tongs 'n Ah'll make yuh anythin' from er spike t'er two-wheel river. . . .

> Any man who says "can't" don't belong on this ilun'.[9]

The conviction that hard work and diligence will yield an abundance of wordly benefits is made evident by Ward's set description for Act II—the description of the island after the freedmen had been working on it for several months:

> The scene is the same, only now the soft tone of fall lends a warmth and a rich sense of harvest. The Freedmen are ginning their cotton, bailing it, and setting it outside for shipment to the mainland. Through earth and industry they have reaped a bountiful crop and an unsuppressable job [sic] bespeaks their realization that they have in their hands now, complete and undeniable, the economic means to guarantee their new life.[10]

It is interesting to note that in this most enthusiastic portrayal of hardworking blacks, the work that is being done is a collective project. A sense of this collectivism and conservatism, although not demonstrated again with such unmitigated enthusaism, does help shape and inform some of the major black dramas of the 1960s.

Over and above its importance as the most sucessful play ever written by a black playwright, Lorraine Hansberry's *A Raisin in the Sun* is important because it is a serious and largely successful attempt to come to grips in a single play with a variety of attitudes and ambivalences that mark black people's views of working in urban, industrialized "white America." Walter Lee Younger's father has died and left the family ten thousand dollars through an insurance policy. Although it is not enough to finance all of the family's dreams, it is enough to get a start on one or two. It is this necessity for choosing among those dreams that allows Hansberry to give voice to a variety of attitudes about how blacks at the dawn of the 1960s perceived their economic position in society. Lena (Mama, Walter's mother) wants to make a down payment on a home so that her family can have the stability and pride of ownership it had never known.[11] Lena and Benethea, Walter's twenty-year-old sister, want the balance to be put aside for Benethea's medical school education. But Walter Lee, resentful of the sacrifices he and his wife have made for the family as low-paid chauffeur and maid, wants to invest with his friends in a liquor store. His dream is to make a fortune like the "white boys" he sees from his boss's limousine. Although he seems to succumb to the "sin" of speculation, Hansberry does not fault him for his desire for quick wealth. As Bigsby and others have pointed out, Hansberry recognizes that Walter is desperate to assert his manhood and to establish a sense of himself:

> I open and close doors all day long. I drive a man around in his limousine an' say "yes sir," "no sir," "very good, sir." "Shall I take the drive, sir." Mama, that ain't no kind of job . . . that ain't nothin' at all . . . . Sometimes it's like I can see the future stretched out in front of me—just as plain as day. The future, mama, hangin' over there at the edge of my days. Just waiting for me—a big looming blank space—full of *nothing*. But it don't have to be.[12]

The case against Walter's investment is a strong one. His mother asserts her powerful traditional values, arguing that the family has always been a family of working people and was not meant to be in business. Moreover, she is dead set against the selling of liquor, which offends her religious upbringing and her belief in the virtue of sobriety. Ruth, Walter's wife, is suspicious of the slick friends with whom Walter wishes to invest. Benethea, who has become quite arrogant while at college, finds Walter's dream of going from chauffeur to entrepreneur laughable. But, as we have seen in *Waiting for Lefty* and *Death of a Salesman,* the frustration of job failure has put such a strain on the male breadwinner's sense of his own identity that the entire family suffers. In order to relieve that tension in Walter and in the rest of the household, Lena reluctantly hands over to Walter the sixty-five hundred dollars that was left over after the down payment on a house.

When Walter finally gets the freedom to assert himself and to make his "deal," he fails. Like Willy Loman, Walter is an outsider to the world of success, and he is compelled to interpret the formula for success from his narrow, outsider's perspective. From that perspective he infers that success comes not from work but from the passing of fortunes back and forth among friends over lunch and other congenial social occasions. Moreover, he believes that deals are cemented by buying off state licensing and inspection officials. Acting on this "knowledge," he turns over the money to one of his partners, who has announced his plans to go to the state capital and "spread it around." Of course, the partner absconds with the entire fortune.

The news of the stolen money practically destroys the family. Lena can barely forgive her son or herself for allowing the fruits of her husband's life of labor to be thrown away on an immoral scheme. Benethea, enraged at the loss of her medical school money, mocks Walter bitterly: "There he is. *Monsieur le petit bourgeois noir— himself.* . . . Did you dream of yachts on Lake Michigan, brother." And Walter is on the verge of discarding all vestiges of decency, honesty, and morality, in a bitter response to his own ignorance:

> It's all divided up . . . between the takers and the "tooken." . . . We get to lookin' around for the right and the wrong and we worry about it and cry about it and stay up nights tryin' to figure it out about the wrong and the right of things all the time—and all the time, man, them takers is out there operating. Just taking and taking.[13]

But just as Theodore Ward rescued Silas Greer, who had no hope of attaining any dignity through work, Lorraine Hansberry rescues Walter Lee. At the end of the play Walter Lee leads the family in resisting a white neighborhood association that wants to move them out of their new home in a predominantly white suburb. As the representative shows up for the final confrontation, Walter rises to the occasion and chases the man off to the resounding cheers of the family. Both his pride and his morality have been restored.

A Raisin in the Sun is an important play as an exploration of the complexity and variety of attitudes about work that are reflective of black life in modern America. It examines differences between older rural blacks and younger urban blacks, the tensions between educated and uneducated blacks, and it presents a credible picture of a crisis in self-image among black males, which, sociologists tell us, is largely the result of the paucity of black males in meaningful, well-paying jobs. But the play cheats itself in that it does not fully come to grips with the very question of jobs and economics that it raises, namely, how do blacks survive economically or psychologically with their own job failure: how will blacks cope with the cynicism of Walter Lee, the bitterness of Benethea, or the sense of loss suffered by Lena when their slight and fragile financial gains dissolve in a single mistake? In economic terms, Hansberry's answer is wholly unsatisfactory.[14] Although race pride restores the family's morale, Walter is still a frustrated chauffeur, his wife is still a maid, his sister has no money for medical school, and they have lost 65 percent of their assets. The play seems to sugarcoat the very serious problems it raises by turning into an uplifting drama of racial pride after presenting the central conflicts in economic and work-related terms.

Far more satisfying in this regard is Lonne Elder III's *Ceremonies in Dark Old Men* (1965). Thirty-year-old Adele works downtown as a secretary to support her father, Russell, and her two brothers Theo, twenty-four, and

Bobby, seventeen. Bobby, Theo, and Russell all spend their days hanging around their Harlem apartment. In the meantime Adele has become bitter about supporting them and has grown fearful that she will work herself to death at an early age, much as her mother had done.

The three men are caught in a crisis that places their sense of pride in conflict with their economic positions. Russell is fearful of looking for work in a white man's world. A former circuit dancer, he tried to find normal work when his legs gave out, but the humiliation was too much for him. ("I am too old a man to ever dream I could overcome the dirt and the filth they got waiting for me down there.")[15] Theo has a strong sense of race consciousness, even though it prevents him from making anything of himself:

> Is it right that all that's down there for us is to go downtown and push one of them carts? I have done that an I ain't gon' do that no more.[16]

Bobby has been developing into a competent, small-time shoplifter, an occupation that gives him spending money and a growing measure of respect in the Harlem neighborhoods.

But for all their fears and resentment of work, the men believe in the moral value of work and accept the fact that it is unethical for them not to work when they can:

> Adele. Can't you understand, Father? I can't go on fore-ever supporting three grown men. *That ain't right.*
> Mr. Parker. (*Shaken by her remarks*) No, it's not right. It's not right at all.[17]

Elder seems to be saying that black males are caught in a dilemma much like Walter Lee Younger's: they accept the rightness and virtue of working and establishing oneself economically; however, they cannot accept the humiliation of jobs that offer low pay, menial tasks, and no future. Moreover, this dilemma is compounded by the false promises of economic and social status that illegal activity holds out to black men. The Parker men embrace this false hope.

Faced with an ultimatum from Adele to get work or leave the apartment, Theo contacts a Harlem criminal (symbolically named Blue Haven), who hires Theo to make corn liquor in the back room of the apartment while Haven uses the place as a front for numbers running and a variety of other illegal schemes.[18] Unknown to Theo, Haven has also hired Bobby to work with a gang of thieves who will conduct large-scale thefts from white-owned businesses in Harlem. But as the irony in Blue Haven's name suggests, life in the rackets proves not to be the panacea the Parkers assumed it would be. Theo soon finds himself stuck in his back room making corn liquor fourteen hours a day. Eventually his complaints echo those of the long-suffering Adele—the protests of a person working for a family that will not work for itself:

> Theo [to Bobby]. I don't like standing over that stove all day. . . . I don't like [Blue] promising me helpers that don't show up. . . . I make the whiskey, I sell it, I keep the books, and *I don't like you standing around here all day not lifting a finger to help me.*[19]

Theo's anguish intensifies when he learns later that Bobby has become a big-time thief in Harlem.

For Bobby's part, the dangerous, illegal activity is a dream coming true. The large sums of money, the short hours, and the immense amount of respect he is getting in his community have made him entirely oblivious to the dangers in his profession and the further erosion of his family. He is, after all, by every superficial measure, a success. Moreover Russell Parker, unaccustomed to having money, is stealing from the business and gallivanting around Harlem with a girl who works for one of Blue Haven's rival thugs.

Seeing that the gangsterism he has brought into his home is destroying the family members both individually and collectively, Theo makes a pact with Adele to make peace, to get out of the rackets, and to work to keep the family unified, respectable, and free from danger.

There are important similarities between *Ceremonies* and *Raisin*. Elder and Hansberry both explore some of the complicated tensions surrounding poor, urban blacks and their struggle to cultivate a working life in America. Moreover, the heroes created by both Hansberry and Elder evolve into what Levine has called the "moral hard man," a traditional hero in black folklore who never preys upon his own people and who wins triumphs within the legal framework of his society.[20] Both authors imply, moreover, that the rejection black men suffer in the white working world places enormous pressures on black women, who then overwork to compensate for those pressures and thus build up resentments of their own.

But unlike Hansberry, Elder offers no sentimental solution to the economic crossfire in which many urban blacks find themselves. There is no ten-thousand-dollar insurance policy, and there is no nervous white neighborhood association representative who cowers in the face of solidarity. Elder suggests that those blacks who are faced with the choice of menial jobs or illegal jobs are being asked to choose between two types of self-destruction, either through humiliation or through violence. He seems to suggest that although the traditional work ethic is a just and valid belief, it is a meaningless standard for judging people who are in no position to garner rewards, be they spiritual or material, for the work they do.

But through the reconciliation of Theo and Adele and their promise to work for each other and respect each other, Elder holds out the possibility for poor urban blacks to establish themselves economically. His philosophy of working to keep the family together, as opposed to working for a white boss or a black thug, is offered to remove the pain of the dilemma that paralyzes many urban blacks. But he is not so optimistic as to think that blacks can reach that accommodation with an ethic of hard, legal work without paying a price to a society that is hostile to black advancement. Indeed, the Parkers' new strength and commitment to work is to be built on Bobby Parker's dead body.

Although *A Raisin in the Sun* and *Ceremonies in Dark Old Men* were among the best and most widely acclaimed black dramas ever written, the increasing militancy of black dramas in the latter half of the 1960s seemed to date their points of view rather quickly.[21] The idea of blacks struggling to accommodate their lives to meet the pressures of white society became to many black playwrights an unthinkable and unspeakable approach to black life, even if some of those "accommodationist" dramas accurately portrayed the hostility of white society. More popular among many black playwrights by 1965 were angry agitprops and satires that portrayed blacks as profoundly and sometimes violently at odds with white people, white values, and white ethics.[22] No play demonstrates the clash of values between black militancy and the protestant work ethic as effectively as does Douglas Turner Ward's satire *Happy Ending* (1966).

Vi and Ellie are domestics in the household of the wealthy Harrisons. The play opens as they return home from work one day weeping because the Harrisons are having domestic difficulties and may get a divorce. Their nephew, Junie, a proud young man filled with the new spirit of racial pride, chides his aunts for feeling sorry for the Harrisons and their petty difficulties. The crying reminds him of the subservient, stereotyped black mammies in *Gone with the Wind*, who cried every time "Missy" had a hangnail:

> Don't get me wrong. I'm not blamin' you for being domestics. It's an honorable job. It's the only kind available sometimes and it carries no stigma in itself—but that's all it is. A JOB! An exchange of work for pay. BAD PAY AT THAT. Which is all the more reason why you shouldn't give a damn if the Harrisons kick, kill, or mangle each other.[23]

But Vi's and Ellie's defense of their actions undercut the expectations of both Junie and the audience. Instead of crying because of the misery suffered by these "good white folks," Vi and Ellie are crying because they might lose their meal ticket—and what a meal ticket it is. Although they are paid low wages, Vi and Ellie have been stealing jewelry, money, clothing, food, and appliances from the Harrisons for years. Moreover Ellie, who manages the Harrisons' books, slips her own bills in with the Harrisons' bills. When Junie realizes that he might lose his source of fine clothing and have to get a job, he joins his aunts in their crying. As the play ends, a call comes from the Harrisons informing the domestics that the marriage has been saved and asking the two women to return to work. Junie closes the play with this revolutionary toast: "To the victors and the vanquished. Top dog and bottom dog. Sometimes it is hard to tell which is which."[24]

The relevance of this play to the question of work attitudes is found in Ellie's justification for her larcenous activities:

> Total it up for nine years and I'd be losin' money on any other job. Now Vi and I after cutting cane, picking cotton, and shuckin corn befo' we could braid our hair in pigtails figure we just gettin' back what's owed us.[25]

Ellie's defense of her thefts reflects the justification that, according to Genovese, slaves used for stealing from their masters. In his chapter "Roast Pig Is a Wonderful Delicacy, Especially When Stolen," Genovese says that slaves justified stealing on the grounds that since they too were property they could scarcely steal other property—they just converted it from one form of property to another. Less clever, but more credible, are the justifications on the grounds that theft of food from the planter not only compensated the slave for the labor he or she expended in its production but also provided the slaves with an essential supplement to the often inadequate rations of food supplied to them.[26]

Also cutting across the bourgeois value of individual responsibility for one's own fate is Ellie's belief that whites are collectively responsible for paying off each other's debts; the sins of one white person are easily compensated for by taking revenge against another. Ellie views the white characters as many black characters in militant dramas do: as allegorical representations of all whites or white society in general.[27]

Ellie and Vi are heroines in the African and Afro-American tradition of the "trickster"—an animal or a slave who by guile and cunning turns the tables on a stronger adversary. The vast popularity and large number of these tales in slave culture speak eloquently to the fact that blacks as a whole never accepted the justifications that the masters put forth in defense of the "peculiar institution." But the prevalence of the trickster in much contemporary black literature suggests perhaps that Ward and other like-minded writers believe that many blacks are not much closer to embracing or being embraced by white values and white systems of work than they were a century ago.

This alienation of blacks from white value systems was, of course, most blatantly and forcefully expressed in the revolutionary dramas of the 1960s. Concerned more with expressing rage and exhorting their audiences to revolutionary action than with analyzing contemporary social conditions, a few plays did single out work and work values as part of the alien, hostile, oppressive system that had to be destroyed if black people were to be free. In *The Great Goodness of Life (A Coon Show)* LeRoi Jones subjects Court Royal, a hard-working, self-consciously middle-class black, to a surrealistic kangaroo court, in which he is accused of the murder of Malcolm X, Medgar Evars, and "dead nigger kids killed by police." His defense is his lifetime record of hard work and achievement: "I have money, I work in the post office, I'm a supervisor."[28] His attorney, a successful black lawyer, is a monstrosity who crawls across the stage in a tuxedo with a wire attached to his back and a large key stuck on the side of his head. The condemnation of blacks who pursue middle-class life in America is uncompromising and unrelenting. It also seems to have hit its target. Clayton Riley writes that a white reviewer, stunned by the laughter of the black audience in response to Royal's repeated reference to his prestigious position with the postal service, reportedly remarked, "There is something about post offices that amuses black people." [29]

A broader but no less caustic condemnation of bourgeois American society in general, and the working life of American blacks in particular, can be found in Archie Shepp's *Junebug Graduates Tonight* (1967). On the day that Junebug ("Junie"), a seventeen-year-old black youth, is to graduate as high school valedictorian (the first high-school graduate in his family's history), other members of his family speak with cynicism of their own futile working lives and of the hopeless future that awaits them. With a bitterness reminiscent of Mrs. Warren's address to her daughter, Junie's mother, Jessie, recalls:

> Every day my man used to go out into the ditch through all seasons and when he came home there would be substance in his eyes from the wind. His hands would be bleedin' from the pick axe and his teeth started to drop out. When he beat me, I cried not out of anger at him but at what made him beat me. The ignorance of a lifetime. [30]

Jessie's bitterness has been passed on to her daughter, who reveals her cynicism as she speaks about her plans to be successful:

> One day I'll take a big, tall cracker whose got millions to burn. My babies will drive Rolls Royces for wagons . . . I know that my dress is torn and that the white girls laugh. What fixes a dress? It takes bread. [31]

While his sister and mother set the tone of the play, Junebug contemplates his upcoming speech. He is in doubt about whether or not to urge his people to accept or reject "the system." What little suspense that surrounds his decision is dispelled quickly in an exchange between Junebug and his blonde girlfriend, America:

> Junebug: Your throat is beautiful in the moonlight. I want to rape it. I'm a black dracula and you are a lonely white throat. . .
> America: I could take you home, put you in a nice warm bed. Fill your belly. Why you could even be a borough president . . . You could take a church . . . Oh can't you see it Reverend Junebug . . . come unto me all you that labor and are heavy laden and I will give you the wind . . . at a price.[32]

Junebug's valedictory speech is, of course, a caustic call for revolution, ending with an onstage explosion that kills both America and Junebug. The scene is a bitter parody of the final scene of *Romeo and Juliet*, but Shepp rather nicely ameliorates some of the play's bitterness by having Junebug say in his dying breath, "I honestly tried to love her."

In the wide range of political viewpoints and dramatic styles that one finds in black drama of the 1960s, at least one point of view remains consistent through almost every play; that whites, specifically middle-class and upper-middle-class whites, are fully adjusted to the jobs they hold and the values of work to which they adhere. If whites have any societal problem at all in these plays, it seems to be how they are to deal with the aspirations of the black characters. Unlike recent black fiction writers who, admittedly, work in a more flexible, relatively uncompressed art form, many black playwrights have oversimplified the working life of whites in their largely successful efforts to examine the complexities that confront the working life of American blacks. The lack of attention to the working problems of the "other race" is certainly reciprocated, however, in the work of white dramatists. In the 1960s and before, conflicts between white, middle-class workers and their work have been generally portrayed as conflicts that isolate people from each other.

The issue of how postwar middle-class work alienates people from one another was posed rather neatly in Herb Gardner's comedy *A Thousand Clowns* (1961). Ostensibly a broad lampooning of various middle-class achievers by way of witty putdowns from hero Murray Burns, the play offers the hypothesis that love and companionship flourish normally when people do not have to work in a phony, glad-handing world of middle-class competition and, conversely, that love and companionship die in the hands of bureaucratic routine and fierce ambition.

The Welfare Department of New York City threatens to take from Murray his beloved nephew Nick if Murray, by choice an unemployed gag writer, does not provide "a wholesome environment" for the child by getting a job. The irony in the play is, of course that one is more likely to provide a wholesome environment for a child if one leaves work, stays home, and plays with him. Fearful of losing the boy if he does not find work, Murray is equally fearful of destroying the boy's spirit if the world of work is permitted to invade their home and their lives:

> I didn't spend six years with him so he should turn into a list maker. He'll learn to know everything before it happens, he'll learn to plan, he'll learn to be one of the nice, dead people.[33]

The issue is too dense for the comedy to resolve, and Gardner offers an unsatisfying, although ultimately realistic, compromise: Murray takes a job, keeps the boy, but will live out his days thumbing his nose at the working stiffs he has finally joined.

But the fullest treatment of the white, middle-class working world of the 1960s came from that decade's two most successful playwrights, Neil Simon and Edward Albee. Concerned not at all with poverty or labor, Simon and Albee staked out the values, ambitions, hypocrisies, and work attitudes of a solvent, even affluent white America. Curiously enough, the two authors held some similar views about middle-class society and its values, although certainly these similarities were manifested in very different dramatic styles.

Although Neil Simon's comedy is very much in the tradition of George S. Kaufman's situation-cum-wisecrack humor, his material is very particular to the decade in which he wrote. While his plots and settings did not often reflect a society in a state of uncertainty and upheaval, his characters certainly did. Throughout the 1960s Simon specialized in comedies of incompatibility, wherein people with violently conflicting and mutually exclusive values were forced by blood, love, sex, or circumstance to adjust to each other. In three of his most important plays, conflicts surrounding work in the contemporary world were at the center of the larger conflict between people with conflicting philosophies of life.

Come Blow Your Horn (1961), Simon's first play, featured themes found in *The Glass Menagerie*, namely conflicts surrounding parents' and grown children's attitudes about work, conformity, and self-fulfillment. Buddy, a twenty-two-year-old who dreams of being a playwright, finds his life as an employee of his father's plastic fruit company too confining. The fact that he also lives at home makes the situation altogether unbearable, and so he decides to move out. The play opens as he arrives unannounced at the apartment of his brother Alan, a thirty-four-year-old lovable con man who survives as a slick-talking salesman for his father's business. Like the hero in the "office farce," Alan has the ability to soft-soap his father and his father's customers while preventing them from ever speaking to one another. This skill has rewarded him with a life of five-day weekends, gloriously excessive womanizing, and precious little responsibility. The comedy emerges as Alan successfully instructs the naïve Buddy in the art of becoming a nonworking gigolo. But once Alan has created his monster, he sees before him his own miserable, irresponsible reflection. Shocked into reality, he quickly proposes to his favorite girlfriend and swears himself to a life of diligent, hard work at his father's plastic fruit business.

As the brothers dislodge one another from their values and move each other toward new values, familiar conflicts in attitudes toward work emerge. When Buddy tries to convince his father that he needs a fulfilling career, he finds his father as intractable in his adherence to asceticism as did Tom Wingfield find Amanda:

> Buddy. Dad, I never had a chance to try anything else [besides the army and the wax fruit business]. I had two years of college, the army, then right into the business. Maybe it's not the right field for me.
> Father. Not the right field. (*He addresses an imaginary listener.*) I give the boy the biggest artificial fruit manufacturing house in the East, and he tells me it's *not the right field*. Ha! That's a hot one.
> Buddy. I don't know if I've got any talent, but I've always toyed with the idea of becoming a writer. . . . Supposing I could write plays for television or for the theater?
> Father. Plays can close. Television you turn off. Wax fruit lays in the bowl until you're a hundred.
> Buddy. But business doesn't stimulate me. I don't have any fun.
> Father. You don't have any fun? I'll put music in, you can dance while you work.[34]

Alan, in turn, gets into an argument with his traditionalist father—not about joyless work but about the amount of work that constitutes a respectable, diligent effort:

> Father. I understand you work very hard. Two days a week and a five day weekend. . . . My own son. I get more help from my competitors.
> Alan. Well, why not? You treat me like one.
> Father. *I* treat you. Do I take three hours for lunch . . . in night clubs. Do I wander in at eleven o'clock in the morning? Do whatever you like and live like a bum.[35]

What is at stake here, of course, is the survival of the father's premodern work values, which are being assaulted by Buddy's hip adolescent quest for self-fulfillment at the expense of "respectable" work and by Alan's hedonistic devotion to leisure and play. But as in the case of most Simon comedies, the clash of values ends in a delightful and thoroughly implausible standoff. Alan finally pleases his father by landing a big account for the business, a success he achieves by introducing the customer to a few of his legions of girlfriends. This impresses Alan's father, who makes up with the now reformed bachelor. Alan agrees to settle down and show up at work by 8:15, but the younger Buddy has taken over the life of the hedonistic bachelor playboy.

Similar conflicts about work arise in *Barefoot in the Park* (1963), the story of Paul Bratter, an ambitious, driven, hardworking, sensible young attorney, and Corie Bratter, his free-spirited, sexy, spontaneous, irresponsible young wife. The plot, such as it is, concerns a running conflict that opens when Paul lands his first case on the same day that Corie rents for them a bohemian and totally unacceptable apartment. What follows is a predictable collision between sex and success:

> Paul. I've got a case in court tomorrow morning. *I've got my first case.*
> Corie. What about tonight?
> Paul. I'll have to go over the briefs. . . . (He hugs Corie.) Oh Corie baby I'm going to be a lawyer.
> Corie. That's wonderful. I just thought we were going to spend the night together.
> Paul. We'll spend tomorrow night together. I hope I brought those affidavits.
> Corie. I brought a black lace nightgown.
> Paul. It looks simple enough. A furrier is suing a woman for non-payment of bills.
> Corie. I was going to put on a record and do an authentic Cambodian fertility dance.
> Paul. The trouble is he didn't have a signed contract.[36]

The lack of communication finally leads to a clash over the value of a rigid life against the value of a spontaneous, undisciplined one. But, like so many Simon characters, Paul and Corie are endearing in their ability to discard their principles for the sake of compatability. When Paul wins his case but is awarded only six cents in damages, he begins to question and reject his ambition and his work ("Work like a dog for six lousy cents"). His despondency seems to make him all the more serious, sober, and rigid. When, in the final act, a frustrated Corie threatens to leave him because he is a "stuffed shirt. . . unable to have a good time," Paul storms out of the house, gets drunk, and runs through the park barefooted in an attempt to become the spontaneous free spirit Corie wants him to be. When he returns, Corie is horrified to see Paul drunk and cries for the hardworking stiff she knew and loved. Paul, his principles and personality malleable to the end, returns to his rigid, hardworking self by the simple act of sobering up. Paul and Corie pledge their love to one another, which is to be manifested in their newly found tolerance of one another.

Although Simon raises some of the same crucial questions about work values that are raised by Miller, Williams, and others, he diffuses the social commentary of his early plays by endowing his characters with an unbelievable ability to tolerate violent offenses to their natures. This tolerance becomes apparent as the characters abandon their values when confronted by anything that resembles a challenge to those values. Their wit notwithstanding, Alan, Buddy, Father Paul, and Corie all take serious risks when they do battle with their families; at stake are life-long relationships with parents, siblings, and spouses to say nothing of careers and money. But Simon dissolves the crises by amicably balancing all conflicts in a world of benign mutual acceptance, as if conflicts in personal values can be reconciled so long as all parties to the conflict can maintain a sharp banter. At the end, souls are never crushed; they simply scrunch over to make room for their opposite and mutually exclusive numbers.

Simon's rather light-headed, if entertaining, approach to human conflict is sustained through most of his comedies, whether they are work related or not. But in *The Prisoner of Second Avenue* (1970), he introduces a character who is not at war with an intractable, wisecracking relative but is instead at war with modern urban society and his own inability to survive it. Although he too is a wisecracking character in the Neil Simon mold, Mel Edison is a man in deeply serious trouble. His anger and bitterness rival those of any character from our most serious dramas.

The play opens in the middle of the night as Mel, a forty-seven-year-old advertising executive in New York City, is having a severe anxiety attack:

> Edna. What is it?
> Mel. I'm unravelling. . . . I'm losing touch.
> Edna. You haven't been sleeping well lately.
> Mel. I don't know where I am half the time. I walk down Madison Avenue, I think I'm in a foreign country.
> Edna. I know the feeling, Mel.
> Mel. It's not just a feeling, something is happening to me. I'm losing control. I can't handle things anymore. The telephone on my desk rings seven, eight times before I answer it.[37]

As Mel begins to focus on the specific sources of his difficulties, we find that he has started to question every decision he has ever made: living in New York, having a family, moving into a "convenient" apartment, spending money on things he does not need, and investing his entire working life in a firm that has absolutely no sense of loyalty to him:

> Edna. What about getting two weeks off. Can't you ask them for two weeks off?
> Mel. Yes, I can ask them for two weeks off. What worries

me is that they'll ask me to take the other fifty weeks as
well.

Edna. You? What are you talking about? You've been
there twenty-two years. Is that what's bothering you?
You're worried about losing your job?

Mel. I'm not worried about losing it. I'm worried about
keeping it. Losing it is easy.[38]

As Edna probes him further, we learn that Mel's company
is in trouble and the chaos and paranoia that a bad year
has caused at the office have worked their way into Mel's
mind. Just as Mel had described his own unraveling, he
describes a parallel unraveling of normal business life at
the office:

The Company lost three million dollars this year. Suddenly they are looking to save pennies. The vice-president
in my department has been using the same paper clip
for three weeks now. A sixty-two year old man with a
duplex on Park Avenue and a house in Southampton running around the office screaming, "Where's my paper
clip."[39]

Mel is also brooding with the fear that Willy Loman has
placed in the minds of all middle-aged working people
who need their employer more than their employer needs
them:

Edna. What if they did fire you? We'd live. You'd find
another job somewhere.

Mel. Where? I'm forty-seven years old in January. They
could get two twenty-three and a half year olds for half
my money . . . And what would I do for a living? Become
a middle-aged cowboy rounding up the elderly cattle.[40]

While Simon had presented problems with work
rather offhandedly in *Barefoot in the Park* and *Come Blow
Your Horn*, this time he does not pull his punches. Mel
is fired, his apartment is robbed of everything in it, and he
has a nervous breakdown. Edna gets a job to support them
while Mel goes through his less-than-promising recovery
period; he goes for walks in the park and plays baseball

with ten-year-olds. Edna then loses her job and the two of them have to beg from Mel's despicable sisters and brother. The play ends comically but with some ominous undertones, unusual for a Simon play. Gradually Mel emerges from the fatigued docility brought on by the breakdown to a state of typical New York angst—yelling at his neighbors and screaming out the window at the city at large. It is at once the survival method by which New Yorkers cope with New York and also evidence of the same symptoms that signaled his breakdown in the first place. Like a surgeon in a combat hospital, Simon cures Mel only to send him into a hopeless battle all over again. Mel is still broke, still abandoned by the system, and still the victim of society's incomprehensible brutality.

In all three of these plays we see some of the same sensibilities toward modern working life that we had seen in *Death of a Salesman* or *The Glass Menagerie*: the pressure that a crisis at work exerts upon the home, the necessity for making specific choices about the kind of working life one will lead, and the notion that bureaucratic society thwarts individual ambition are all there. But we do not see the emotional intensity of these earlier plays, nor do we see a directed probing of people caught in social crises. Instead, Simon seems to have responded to the apparent political chaos of the 1960s by embuing his frantic, fast-talking characters with a similarly unstructured sense of values. Mel is as likely to pound on the wall in order to silence his neighbor as to rail against his boss, convinced that the two are one and the same enemy. Corie Bratter berates her husband with equal vigor for wearing gloves in winter and for ignoring her advances. In *Come Blow Your Horn*, Buddy and Alan exchange values so quickly that it is impossible to understand the motivations behind Alan's instant transformation to the wax apple of his father's eye.

What concerns Simon, it seems, is not so much the implications that a crisis holds for an individual's psychology as for his *lifestyle*—a pastiche of attitudes and activities encompassing work, sex, politics, and self-discipline. But unlike Marxism, Puritanism, or other ordered value systems, the lifestyle of Simon's characters is like the popular image of the 1960s themselves: a blinding collage filled with jagged edges and strong lines, in which major considerations are indistinguishable from minor considerations. It allows Simon's characters to cast off their values and to assume new ones without even breaking comic timing, much less disrupting character consistency. It also allows for Simon's comic lines to advance the story rather than to disrupt it; his wisecrackers can deflate issues of great pith, and his mad ranters can elevate the trivial. There is no clear-cut sense of proportion to be preserved. Simon's world is like that aspect of the 1960s that seemed to suspend permanent values in a perpetual state of impermanence, lacking as it does a secure place upon which to fix those values. To that extent Simon's comic vision of America is not far removed from that of the most serious American playwright of the decade, Edward Albee.

By his own admission, Albee is a dramatist who produces "the same effects" as a social critic. Yet his social criticism rarely centers on the popular issues of his times. Rather he embraces the radicalism of his society in his anger at and rejection of the phoniness he sees in bourgeois attitudes about life. In an age of mass politics, Albee strives for intimacy in his plays. But his intimate scenes can become so abstract that often the social significance of these plays, to say nothing of the storyline itself, can become difficult and confusing. In his introduction to *The American Dream*, for example, Albee clearly sets out the political and social message of the play. But the issues he is attacking involve the politics of human interaction and self-image in American society—a curious and highly unconventional form of politics in or out of the theater:

> The play is an examination of the American Scene, an attack on the substitution of artificial for real values in our society, a condemnation of complacency, cruelty, emasculation, and vacuity; it is a stand against the fiction

that everything in this slipping land of ours is peachy-keen.[41]

This examination of America is undertaken through a searing personal dialogue in which Albee's detached and passionless characters "strip themselves of all pretense" in their effort "to survive as autonomous individuals and accept their responsibility toward other people."[42] In fact the theatricality and the politics of most of Albee's plays are derived from this frightening process by which people are forced to confront values and commitments that their untroubled bourgeois existences have betrayed. If Albee has inherited his political commitment from Americans like Rice, Odets, or Miller, he has developed the artistry and philosophy of his political drama from Beckett, Ionesco, and Genet.

In his well-known essay "Which Theater Is the Absurd One?" Albee explains that he and the other so-called absurdist playwrights (a label he toys with rather skillfully in the essay) intend to free their audiences from the illusion that the moral, political, religious, and social structures that man has erected for the purpose of giving meaning and order to his existence are still functioning, if indeed they ever functioned at all. Thus the constant struggle of men, possessed of the illusion that they can accommodate their lives to fit those structures (or accommodate those structures to fit their lives), is seen by absurdist playwrights as a continuous exercise in futility—an absurd existence, if you will.

Frustrated and appalled by the tendency of modern men and women to deceive themselves in this manner, Albee, Beckett, and others are at least as angered by the notion that a play, in order to "make it" to Broadway or to win acceptance by an audience raised on "realism," must participate in this deception by re-enforcing values that, he argues, do not even exist. Thus, it is the absurdist drama that is "realistic" in that it confronts reality, and it is realism that is absurd in that it surrenders to the non-

sense of modern life and portrays it as if it were meaningful and purposeful.[43]

However, at one point Albee does part company with
his European colleagues and enters into the tradition, if
not the ranks, of American social dramatists. As Bigsby
has observed, Albee sees the absurdity and powerlessness
of man to be "of man's own making" and not the product
of an indifferent, infinite void of a universe.[44] Therefore,
even if his social drama is far more abstract than the
realism and modified naturalism that characterize most
social drama in America, Albee is neither unaware of nor
uninterested in conventional political and social issues.
Tension between the sexes, conformity and its emascula-
ting effects on middle-class men, and the intellectual and
moral bankruptcy of middle-class life are all themes found
in Albee's plays.

And in his attacks on middle-class life, Albee has
thrown more than a glancing blow at American working
life. For example in *The Zoo Story* (1959), the violent
confrontation between Peter, a detached, moderate, and
cautious small-time executive, and Jerry, a hostile and
passionately violent social outcast, Albee assaults the middle class's discomfort with its own working values by
having Jerry interrogate Peter about his life and his work.
Jerry's questions reduce Peter to making guarded and
defensive remarks about his work in an unsuccessful attempt to parry the intensive psychological assault:

> Jerry. And what else? What do you do to support your
> enormous household?
> Peter. I . . . uh . . . I have a small publishing house. We
> . . . uh . . . we publish text books.
> Jerry. I bet you don't know what to make of me do you?
> Peter. (*a joke*) We get all kinds in publishing (chuckles).[45]

As Jerry exposes Peter's fear and discomfort with his job
(as well as with his family, his home, his hobbies, and his
inability to handle the confrontation itself) a terrifying
intimacy develops, ending in Peter unwillingly stabbing

Jerry and Jerry's confounding expression of gratitude for that act.

In *The Zoo Story* Albee presents middle-class working life as being one of several layers of paralysis that prevent meaningful, passionate communication among people. One sees traces of a similar view in the character of the young man in *The American Dream* and to a lesser extent in the old woman in *Quotations from Chairman Mao*. But Albee's view of problems of modern men and modern work assume their most powerful expression in his fullest and most powerful play, *Who's Afraid of Virginia Woolf?* (1961).

Work is vital to this portrait of a marriage because Albee has "wedded it" to the castration of George, the history professor who has been emasculated by his relentlessly cruel wife as well as by his own career misfortunes. As the daughter of George's boss, Martha is both the symbol and the force who merges the two castrating agents of woman and work:

> George. There are easier things in the world if you happen to be teaching at a university, there are easier things than being married to the President's daughter. There are easier things in the world.
> Martha. It should be an extraordinary opportunity . . . for some men it would be the chance of a lifetime . . . Some men would give their right arm for the chance.
> George. Alas, Martha, in reality it works out that the sacrifice is usually a somewhat more private portion of the anatomy.[46]

But George has been as much unmanned by the men with whom he works as by the woman with whom he lives. When George desired to express himself meaningfully, that is, to tell the world the truth about his own life, he wrote a novel about a violent trauma that occurred in his youth. But his father-in-law forced him to bury the manuscript; it was a crippling and humiliating defeat that Martha recalls with relish:

> Martha. [quoting her father]. Why, the idea! A teacher
> at a respected, conservative institution like this, in a
> town like New Carthage, publishing a book like that?
> If you respect your position here, young man, young
> . . . whippersnapper, you'll just withdraw that manu-
> script. . . .[47]

George is also threatened by Nick, the young biology professor who plans to "start a few groups, take over some
courses from the older men, plow a few pertinent wives,"
and then take over the faculty. M.A. at nineteen, Ph.D. at
twenty-two, and collegiate boxing champion, biologist
Nick is the embodiment of an aggressive, ambitious, outer-
directed personality manipulator who challenges both the
sexual and career status of the contemplative, passive historian George.[48] George has also been subdued by other
members of his department who returned to New Carthage after World War II. Unfit for military service, George
headed up the department during the war years. But upon
the return of the other staff members, he surrendered his
position to men who were to become and remain his
superiors.

George is, of course, fully aware of the atrophy of his
career. Having lost the capacity to confront directly his
own sense of loss, he speaks of his subhuman existence
with a detachment that suggests in its misanthropy, if not
in its tone, the same dissipation of the human spirit that
we saw in Mr. Zero in *The Adding Machine*:

> Martha's father expects his . . . staff . . . to cling to the
> walls of this place, like the ivy . . . to come here and grow
> old . . . to fall in the line of service. One man, a professor
> of Latin and elocution, actually fell in the cafeteria line,
> one lunch. He was buried, as many of us have been, as
> many of us will be, under the shrubbery around the
> chapel. It is said . . . that we make excellent fertilizer.[49]

While the contemplative George tries to bury his failure
with his quiet if sardonic detachment, Martha confronts
him with it continuously. With justice he calls this "need-

less cruelty" on her part, but her strident reminder to George of his own failure stands as the simple picture of reality that all working people with failed ambition must live with day after day. A central part of the "exorcism" that occurs in this play is the raising up of the painful truth that confronts everyone whose working life has fallen short of expectations:

> You see, George didn't have much . . . push . . . he wasn't particularly . . . aggressive. In fact he was sort of a . . . Flop . . . who's married to the President's daughter, who's expected to *be* somebody, not just some nobody bookworm, somebody who's so damn . . . contemplative he can't make anything out of himself, somebody without the *guts* to make anybody proud of him.[50]

As Bonin has noted, George, in his passivity, is singularly unsuited for the politics of academic life. But the futility of George's career is evident in the fact that even if he were more successful he would be no happier than he is now.[51] As chairman of the department, he would be even more involved with his loathed father-in-law. As a powerful member of the faculty, he would be more vulnerable to attacks by the young faculty like Nick, and, indeed, would become as empty and hungry as they in his efforts to fight them off. He would still be "clinging" to the walls of New Carthage as desperately as he does now. The only chance he ever had to fulfill himself, to face the truth of his life, was in the writing of his novel, a chance he discarded by choosing instead to toe the line and not publish the work. The futility of George's career, then, does not lie in his lack of aggressiveness but in his decision to fulfill himself by following a career—a career that has led him through a cycle of disappointments and a life of forced self-delusion, neither of which is tied to his ability to cope. To Albee, that is the futility that careers offer to men and women who choose to follow them.

Although Neil Simon and Edward Albee share very little ground as dramatic artists or social critics, they both perceive middle-class society in the 1960s as hostile to permanent meaningful values. For Albee, the void of important human values has caused us to substitute false, meaningless values for them. When these false values are stripped away, as they are in *The Zoo Story, Who's Afraid of Virginia Woolf?*, and *A Delicate Balance*, a sense of loss encompasses the drama: a sense of loss caused by the violent recognition by characters and audience of the emptiness of modern life.

But Neil Simon does not seek to correct the people or the society. He finds in them a wellspring for comedies in which people strain to tolerate the wholly intolerable people and situations in their lives. Although his characters express beliefs in certain "values," we learn that these values are not nearly as permanent as, say, bad habits. We also learn that these values are not worth fighting for; if they were, Paul and Corie Bratter would fight as intensively as George and Martha in *Virginia Woolf*.

In the chaotic 1960s Edward Albee still seeks a level of meaningful communication while Simon delights in its impossibility. Simon seems to say that we are forced to accept the absurdities of our own making; not only must the lion lie down with the lamb, but also the slob with the "neatnik," the playboy with the workaholic, and New Yorkers with New York. Masquerading as celebrations of the liberal virtue of tolerance, Simon's plays have, as much as those of any absurdist, reflected the political and social disorder of the decade.

CONCLUSION

It would be overstating the case to suggest that work forms the thematic or intellectual center of all American drama or even of all American social drama. Major American writers such as Eugene O'Neill, Maxwell Anderson, Ed Bullins, and William Inge have written successful and important plays without paying very much attention to the problem of work or the work ethic in modern society. But we cannot escape the fact that it is a theme that has since the 1920s attracted the attention of many of our finest playwrights, who have in turn culled from that source some of the best and most significant plays ever written in America. The full potential of work as a dramatic theme, which was pioneered for modern American playwrights by Elmer Rice, has been pursued from different approaches by Clifford Odets, Robert Sherwood, Arthur Miller, Tennessee Williams, Paddy Chayefsky, Lorraine Hansberry, Edward Albee, and Neil Simon—certainly an impressive if not entirely definitive list of major American dramatists. If we add to this the dozens of lesser-known dramatists who have made work and work attitudes central themes in their dramas, we begin to see that the theme of work is not merely important as a feature of some few of our most successful plays but is also significant as a wellspring of human and social conflict for any socially aware playwright or play reader.

As we have seen repeatedly in this study, playwrights believe that they have a great deal to teach us about our working lives, and this belief doubtless accounts for much of the attraction that the theme and subject of work hold for American dramatists. Taken en masse, the more important work-related plays tell us as much or more than any other source available to us about the spiritual, psychological, and economic relationships between twentieth-century Americans and their work. For example, by examining the psychological needs of some of the heroes in these plays, we can begin to see in microcosm the rising expectations of an increasingly educated and increasingly prosperous American working man, whose frustrations often appear to increase in direct proportion to his material worth. We see in Joe, the unemployed cab driver in Odets's *Waiting for Lefty*, a man who is desperate for a job so that he can support his wife and two children. This and this alone will serve to fulfill him. However, fifteen years later we meet Willy Loman, who holds a job for thirty-six years and is able to raise his children to adulthood. But Willy is lost and frustrated by his inability to understand the postwar world of upward mobility, in which he finds himself sliding downward. As a struggling member of the middle class, he has achieved more than the threadbare survival that Joe had hoped for, but he has far less dignity and none of the pride that Joe gains from his strike meeting. When we meet George, Edward Albee's history professor, in 1963, we come upon a man who is financially secure and thoroughly knowledgeable about his position in the working world. But in many ways he is the most pathetic of the three. Bright enough to grasp the political forces that operate in the universiy for which he works, his failed ambitions have left him so miserable that he has built up in his work and in his marriage a placid, detached demeanor that masks his seething rage and his immense self-loathing. George is all the more pathetic for his intellect, which forces him to live with the knowledge of his bitter, fradulent existence.

Another dimension of American working life that our playwrights clearly point out is the effect of work on the self-identity of American men, who have historically made up the bulk of the labor force and on whose shoulders has ridden a disproportionate share of the responsibility for upholding society's work values. Contemporary clichés of popular sociology about the pressures of work on male sexuality have been for years presented on the American stage as riveting and frightening truths. One such truth is revealed in the sexual obtuseness of Mr. Zero, whose lifetime of monotonous work in Elmer Rice's *The Adding Machine* has turned his sexual desires into vague and remote daydreams upon which he has no power to act. We also see a crisis in male identity in the self-destructiveness that drives all of the male characters in Elder's *Ceremonies in Dark Old Men*. These men stand with other injured working males we find in such "inspirational" dramas as Rice's *We, the People*, Treadwell's *Hope for a Harvest*, or Hansberry's *A Raisin in the Sun*. In all three of these dramas, men who have been beaten down temporarily by failures in their working lives are restored to their sense of dignity by the encouragement and ingenuity of the stronger and less vulnerable women who love them. Perhaps it is only in heroes' escapes in Williams's *The Glass Menagerie* or in O'Neill's plays of the sea that the yoke of manliness through work is fully removed from the American man.

The weight that is placed upon the shoulders of both working men and women in modern American dramas also stands as evidence of the power and resilience of some of the most traditional aspects of the pre-industrial work ethic, aspects that remain very much alive not only in the plays of those dramatic artists who endorse the work ethic but also in the plays of those who challenge it, satirize it, and abhor it. Traditional, pre-industrial values temper the radicalism of John Howard Lawson, guide the pro-unionist sympathies of Odets, modify the liberalism of Arthur Miller, and diffuse the anger of Lonne Elder III. Even in dramas where work is not the central issue, traditional and presumably "irrelevant" work values loom large over the conflicts at hand, such as in Chayefsky's *Middle of the Night* or Albee's *The Zoo Story*.

Issues of sexual identity, the rising expectations of the white middle class, the endurance of traditional pre-industrial work values in industrial America, racial pride, class consciousness, and other work-related themes discussed in this study all seem to point to a larger question that lies at the center of virtually all serious dramas about work in modern America: namely, how will man establish his dignity and his sense of self-worth in a society where bureaucratic rationalization, personality manipulation, conformity, and mechanization are powerful, immutable forces. It is insufficient to invoke the cliché that work alienates workers; true enough, but the issue is larger than that. It is a question that assumes that society's economic forces, particularly its work, are as important to the destiny of man in modern America as were the Oracle of Delphi or the Furies to the ancient Greeks. It is an assumption that invites plays of human destruction at the hands of these forces (Miller's *All My Sons*), plays of romantic heroism (Sherwood's *The Rugged Path* or Maltz's *Black Pit*), as well as dramas of open defiance of these forces (Rice's *We, the People*).

At its best this collective search for the modern working man's dignity stands as testimony to a drama that is both pragmatic and compassionate. It is a drama that understands the structures of modern society yet speaks to the souls of the people who live in it. Moreover, these plays offer a selflessness and social awareness that balance the sometimes tiresome introspection of a Eugene O'Neill or the gratuitously hip narcissism of a Sam Shepard, while simultaneously offsetting the light-headed entertainments that keep the commercial end of American theater alive. Among the many plays with work-related themes there is a self-conscious attempt to reach out to a society in which everyone either works for a living or relies on someone else who does. Using the universality of work themes that is built into the economic structure of society, these dramatists write plays that are not only tragic, poignant, or humorous, but are also useful and instructive to society.

Conclusion

Through their characters, the authors identify problems, warn of dangers, and even propose solutions to problems we incur in our working lives.

Since problems at work speak so strongly to so many of us, it is not surprising that some of the most important and enduring characters in all American drama have been born of these plays: Willy Loman, Tom and Laura Wingfield, George and Martha of New Carthage, and Walter Lee Younger. Certainly the ready-made universality of work themes has intensified the impact of these characters upon their audiences, an impact that has made these and other characters stand as cultural symbols for various aspects of American working life. This empathy between a society of working audiences and a collection of working characters has given as much to the artistic and social strength of American drama as has any other facet of that literature.

Finally, if modern American drama ever does assume the stature of a great body of drama in Western civilization, it is likely to do so not simply because it has produced an occasional Eugene O'Neill or an occasional *Death of a Salesman*. Accompanying and perhaps surpassing the importance of the brightest stars in the galaxy will be the galaxy itself: scores of playwrights who address themselves to the central issues of their own nation in their own time. Since the world of work and our attitudes toward it are fundamental to the economic, social, emotional, and spiritual life of our people, the drama of work in America stands as one of the strongest foundations upon which is built a growing, and thriving, American dramatic art.

NOTES

INTRODUCTION

1. Indeed, the American dramatists' definition of work is considerably flexible and variable, but no less so than that of the social historians, who understand the complexity of the issues raised by an examination of work and have accommodated themselves nicely to that complexity by loosely defining The Term. In *White Collar*, sociologist C. Wright Mills serves sociology and art very well when he defines work as virtually anything one can associate with it: "Work may be a source of livelihood or the most significant part of one's inner life: it may be experienced as expiation or as exuberant expression of self, or as the development of man's universal nature. Neither love nor hatred of work is inherent in man or inherent in any given line of work, for work has no intrinsic meaning," p. 215.

2. Max Weber, *The Protestant Ethic and the Spirit of Capitalism*.

3. Ibid., p. 51.

4. Mills and Weber both observe further that this personality develops not only out of Protestant religiosity but also out of the needs of burgeoning European capitalism during the Reformation. Weber reminds us that the new Protestant capitalism simply could not tolerate the pre-capitalist ethos of those who had no acquisitive desires and who resisted stubbornly any attempts to increase the productivity of human labor. Thus the "ceaseless, methodical" Protestant is pressed into the service of the new and emerging economic order. See Weber, *The Protestant Ethic*, p. 60.

5. Weber, *The Protestant Ethic*, p. 36.

6. The view of capitalism as a system of increasingly rationalized systems of production and labor is argued most forcefully in Harry Braverman, *Labor and Monopoly Capitol*. He is given considerable support in Daniel Rodgers, *The Work Ethic in Industrial America, 1850–1920*. An interesting counterpoint to these two works is British historian David Montgomery's *Workers Control in America*, which views the American labor movement as a series of responses to capitalism's attempts at rationalized, systemized control of labor.

7. Weber, *The Protestant Ethic*, p. 72.

8. Daniel Rodgers, *The Work Ethic in Industrial America, 1850–1920*, pp. 6–7.

9. E P. Thompson, "Time, Work Discipline and Industrial Capitalism," *Past and Present* 38 (1967): 89.

10. Mills, *White Collar*, pp. 8–9.

11. Braverman, *Labor and Monopoly Capital*, p. 83.
12. Montgomery, *Workers Control*, chapter 1 passim.
13. Braverman, *Labor*, pp. 112–19 passim.
14. Rodgers, *The Work Ethic*, p. 30.
15. Thompson, "Time, Work Discipline," p. 86.
16. The extent of the effort made by some companies to convert their workers from traditional, pre-industrial work habits was often extraordinary. Just prior to World War I, the International Harvester Corporation prepared a brochure to teach its Polish common laborers the English language. An excerpt from Lesson One reads:

> I hear the whistle. I must hurry
> I hear the five minute whistle
> It is time to go into the shop. . .
> I change my clothes and get ready for work.

Herbert G. Gutman, *Work, Culture & Society in Industrializing America*, p. 6.
    At about the same time, the Ford Company hired teams of social workers to examine the daily habits and private lives of their new employees in order to determine how their adjustment to modern life could be most efficiently and swiftly accommodated by the company.
17. Gutman, *Work, Culture & Society in Industrializing America*, p. 15.
18. Rodgers, *The Work Ethic*, p 28.
19. Mills, *White Collar*, p. 100.
20. Michael Crozier, quoted in Mills, *White Collar*, p. 130.
21. Mills, *White Collar*, p. 219
22. Rodgers, *The Work Ethic*, p. xii.
23. Mills, *White Collar*, p. 34.
24. Clark Kerr, *Industrialism and Industrial Man: The Problem of Labor and Management in Economic Growth* (Cambridge, Mass.: Harvard University Press, 1960), p. 43.
25. Ely Chinoy, *Automobile Workers and the American Dream*, pp. 119–22 passim.
26. Alan Dawley and Paul Faler, "Working-Class Culture and Politics in the Industrial Revolution: Sources of Loyalism [*sic*] and Rebellion." *Journal of Social History* 9 (1976): 466.

CHAPTER I

1. Admittedly, the rise of naturalism in American literature is not an entirely separate "tradition" from European naturalist movements, for the former is certainly the child of the latter. But in the evolution of work as a major theme in American drama, the European background and the American background are quite distinct from one another. Thus, two separate discussions are undertaken here with the understanding that there are many common bonds between dramas of early European and American naturalism.
2. Anton Chekhov, *Plays*, trans. Elisaveta Fen (Middlesex: Penguin, 1951), p. 76.

Notes

3. Ibid., p. 96.
4. Ibid., p 240.
5. Ibid., pp. 252–53.
6. Ibid.
7. Ibid , p. 329.
8. Anton Chekhov, *The Cherry Orchard*, in Haskell M. Block and Robert G. Shedd, eds., *Masters of Modern Drama*, p. 205.
9. Ibid., p. 211.
10. Chekhov, *Plays*, p. 203.
11. Ibid., p. 309.
12. Gerhart Hauptmann, *The Weavers*, in Block and Shedd, *Masters of Modern Drama*, p. 133.
13. Ibid., p. 130.
14. Ibid.
15. Ibid., p. 146.
16. Ibid., p. 149.
17. Block and Shedd, *Masters of Modern Drama*, p. 126.
18. Hauptmann, *The Weavers*, p. 149.
19. Maxim Gorki, *Enemies*, trans. Kitty Hunter-Blair (New York: Viking, 1972), pp. 7–8.
20. Ibid., p. 9.
21. Ibid., p. 90.
22. George Bernard Shaw, *Mrs. Warren's Profession*, p. 215.
23. Ibid., pp. 215–16.
24. Garff B. Wilson, *Three Hundred Years of American Drama from "Ye Bear" and "Ye Cubb" to "Hair,"* p. 224.
25. William Pratt, *Ten Nights in a Barroom*, p. 154.
26. Ibid., p. 180.
27. Clyde Fitch, *The City*, in *Representative American Dramas*, ed. Montrose J. Moses (Boston: Little & Brown, 1925), p. 160.
28. Ibid., p. 186.
29. Edward Sheldon, *The Boss*, p. 870.
30. Ibid., p. 882.
31. In her brief but useful essay on "Work and Material Rewards," Jane F. Bonin sees a larger interest in work on O'Neill's part than I do, especially in *Strange Interlude*. However, Bonin does suggest that O'Neill's social concerns are rather abstract, involving the need to transcend "the American Dream" and to attack the ethos of materialism in America. See *Major Themes in Prize-Winning American Drama*, pp. 36–39.

CHAPTER II

1. Elmer Rice, *The Living Theater*, p. 121.
2. Elmer Rice, *Minority Report: An Autobiography*, p. 127.
3. Loren Zeller, in "Two Expressionistic Interpretations of Dehumanization: Rice's *The Adding Machine* and Muniz's El *Tintero*," *Essays in Literature* 2 (1975): 245–55, credits the expressionism in *The Adding Machine* with inspiring the expressionistic technique in the later Spanish play. Zeller also makes use of Frank Durham's brief discussion in *Elmer Rice* (New York: Twayne, 1970) in which Durham notes that the

169

Work and the Work Ethic

theme of "the new man" in struggle against the machine age is found in the works of Georg Kaiser. In William Elwood's "An Interview with Elmer Rice on Expressionism," *Educational Theater Journal* (20 June 1969): 1–7, the author contends that Rice's *The Adding Machine* and *The Subway* may well have been written "with the principles of German Expressionism in mind" in spite of Rice's vigorous denials to the contrary. The most convincing argument for a direct, conscious influence of German expressionism upon *The Ading Machine* may be found in Peter Bauland's *The Hooded Eagle: Modern German Drama on the New York Stage*, p. 92: "*The Adding Machine,* in its *stationen* development of the story of Mr. Zero, in its reduction of characters to types . . . , in its settings of whirling turntables, walls decorated with numbers, and an adding machine over which men crawl, employs every one of the major devices of expressionism even to the extent of artificial dialogue and choral speaking."

4. Rice, *Minority Report,* p. 190.

5. Ibid., p. 199.

6. Ibid., p. 190.

7. Elmer Rice, *Three Plays,* pp. 21–22. The point can be made by historians who argue that modern work has been so devalued as to have no meaning beyond its function as a means by which individuals purchase their leisure that Zero is actually reciting his leisure routine; as he faces death, neither his wife nor his work have meaning to him—only his days off. And Rice renders even these precious days laughably meaningless.

8. Rice, *Three Plays,* p. 54.

9. See Braverman's discussion of the devaluation of the skills of clerical workers as a result of the widespread use of typewriters and adding machines in American business in the first twenty years of this century. *Labor and Monopoly Capital,* pp. 326–48.

10. Rice, *Three Plays,* p. 10.

11. Ibid., p. 61.

12. Burns Mantle, ed., *Best Plays of 1932–1933* (New York: Dodd & Mead, 1933), p. v.

13. A fine discussion of the history of labor and left-wing theater in New York is Morgan Y. Himelstein's *Drama Was a Weapon.* More valuable for its encyclopedic collation of information and description of labor plays than for its thesis (that communists tried and failed to take over legitimate theater in New York during the 1930s), the book discusses in detail the considerable number of interrelated, left-wing theater movements in New York during the depression years.

14. Mantle, p. 133.

15. Richard Dana Skinner, Review of *We the People, The Commonweal* 7 (8 February 1933): 411.

16. Joseph Wood Krutch, Review of *We the People, The Nation* 136: 3527 (8 February 1933): 811.

17. Elmer Rice, *Counselor-at-Law,* quoted in Anthony Palmieri, "Elmer Rice: A Playwright's Vision of America," pp. 153–54.

18. It should be noted that *Street Scene,* Rice's best known and most important social drama, is not discussed at length here because, in my judgment, its subject matter does not involve work but rather the so-

called "working class." This distinction is important because in the rather undefined view of liberal literary criticism, literature about the "working class" has come to mean almost anything involving ethnics in T-shirts. Although concerned with urban poverty, the play offers little in the way of meaningful ideas or attitudes about work.

CHAPTER III

1. Morgan Y. Himelstein in *Drama Was a Weapon* and William Kozlenko in his introduction to *Best Short Plays of the American Social Theatre* see 1930s social drama as a single, isolated movement while Harold Clurman in his introduction to *Famous American Plays of the 1930's* (New York: Dell, 1959) more correctly views the thirties as a "sharpening" of "tendencies" already evident in the 1920s.

2. Lillian Sabine, *The Rise of Silas Lapham*, p. 9.

3. Ibid., p. 49.

4. Ibid., pp. 103–4.

5. See my monograph, "Reality and the Language of Finance in O'Neill's *More Stately Mansions*," *Virginia Union University Monograph Series*, forthcoming.

6. Sophie Treadwell, *Machinal*, in Burns Mantle, ed., *Best Plays of 1928–1929*, pp. 226–27.

7. Elliot Field, *Tenant Farmers* (Boston: Baker, 1939), pp. 17, 21.

8. Warren I. Susman, "The Thirties," in Stanley Coben and Lorman Ratner, eds., *The Development of an American Culture*, pp. 179–218.

9. It is interesting to observe that, while Susman sees the principles of self-reliance and individualism in Carnegie's work as a renewed interest in the values of a pre-industrial society, David Riesman in *The Lonely Crowd* takes a very different position on the importance of Carnegie's work. Riesman argues that Carnegie and other authors of books on self-motivation are the logical products of rationalized, modern society, where success requires that one manipulate one's own personality in order to manipulate the personality of others—a vital skill in a society where division of labor has so removed workers from the end product of their labor that most work involves the manipulation of people rather than the production of goods. Hardly a neo-nineteenth century Puritan, Carnegie represents to Riesman the ethic of social adjustment and "getting along" that pervades social, industrial, and governmental bureaucracies. See Riesman, p. 161.

10. Susman, "The Thirties," p. 205.

11. See also Jane F. Bonin, *Major Themes in Prize-Winning American Drama*, pp. 33 and 39, in which she notes the conservative bent of Sidney Howard's *They Knew What They Wanted* and William Saroyan's *The Time of Your Life*.

12. Mark Reed *Let's Get Rich*, p. 81.

13. Philip Barry, *Holiday*.

14. Ibid., pp. 69–70.

15. Kozlenko, "Introduction," *Best Short Plays*, p. vii.

16. Himelstein defines socialist realism as the "realistic depiction of [Communist] Party fantasies," *Drama Was a Weapon*, p. 59.

17. Himelstein documents the Communist Party press's displeasure with the early radical theater groups in *Drama Was a Weapon*, chapters 1 and 2, passim.

18. In *The Fervent Years* Clurman states specifically that the Group Theater's purpose was not to be an advocate of left-wing politics but rather an experiment in a permanent theater ensemble and an American incubator for the Stanislavski method of acting and directing. Nevertheless, left-wing sympathies abounded among the Group Theater's personnel, causing the Communist Party to infiltrate its ranks in an attempt to wrest power away from its three leaders, Clurman, Cheryl Crawford, and Lee Strasberg. Also, the Group Theater owes much of its enduring reputation in the history of the theater to the work of Clifford Odets, whose profound interest in left-wing themes and ideas has left an indelible radical stamp upon the Group Theater, Clurman's disclaimers notwithstanding.

19. William Kozlenko, *The Earth Is Ours*, p. 260.

20. Clifford Odets, *Waiting for Lefty* p. 52.

21. Clurman, *The Fervent Years*, pp. 147–48.

22. Odets, "Notes on *Waiting For Lefty*," p. 53.

23. Albert Maltz, *Black Pit*, p. 103.

24. Martyrs and traitors to the union cause had been made popular for years in other forms of "labor art," particularly the labor song and labor poem. Songs such as Joe Hill's "Casey Jones—Union Scab" and "Mr. Block" offered no sympathy to anyone who broke the labor alliance for any reason. These songs, which predated the depression by almost twenty years, had clearly worked out the dilemma of individual versus group loyalty long before the advent of the labor drama. For a history of early IWW songs see Joyce Kornbluh, *Rebel Voices: An I.W.W. Anthology*.

25. Susman in "The Thirties" is most helpful in analyzing the conservative underpinnings of radical art and culture in the 1930s.

26. John Howard Lawson, *Marching Song*, p. 95.

27. Paul Green, *The Enchanted Maze* (New York: Samuel French, 1936), pp. 86–87.

28. Leopold Atlas, *But for the Grace of God*, p. 102.

29. Orrie Lashing and Milo Hastings, *Class of '29*, p. 131.

30. Atlas, *For the Grace of God*, p. 37.

31. See Kozlenko, "Introduction," *Best Short Plays*, p. viii ff.

32. Sidney Kingsley, *Men in White*, p. 92 n.

33. Odets, *Three Plays*, pp. 46–47.

34. George Brewer, "Introduction" to *Tide Rising*, pp. 5–9.

35. Brewer, *Tide Rising*, p. 138.

36. Eugene O'Neill, *The Hairy Ape*, p. 71.

37. John Howard Lawson, "Introduction" to *Processional*, in *Contemporary Drama*, eds. E. Bradlee Watson and Benfield Pressey, p. 184.

38. Wilson Whitman, *Bread and Circuses*, pp. 73–90 passim.

39. E. Quita Craig, writing in *Black Drama of the Federal Theatre Era*, p. 64, notes that *Liberty Deferred*, written by Federal Theater staff members John Sivera and Abram Hill, was rejected by Federal Theater for production. This rejection was later cited by the Negro Arts Council in a discrimination suit against the Federal Theater.

Notes

CHAPTER IV

1. Although Arthur Schlesinger, Jr., and other liberal historians argued in the late 1940s and early 1950s that the New Deal and not the war had been responsible for the end of the depression, historians and economists of all political persuasions, including liberals, have come to discredit this argument.

2. Morgan Y. Himelstein, *Drama Was a Weapon*, chapters 9 and 10 passim.

3. John Steinbeck, *The Moon Is Down*, p. 75.

4. Ibid., p. 87.
Lanser's bureaucratic dispatching of his bloodletting is remarkably similar to the portrait we see of Adolph Eichmann in Hannah Arendt's account of his trial in 1961 (*Eichmann in Jerusalem: A Report on the Banality of Evil*). The mountain of legal and procedural dicta that Hitler's lawyers created out of his desire to rid Europe of all its Jews grew into a modern, rationalized bureaucracy: complete with internal office infighting, personality manipulation, and the division of the task into countless, minute operations. Heading the project was the perfect bureaucrat: Adolph Eichmann, an uneducated paper pusher whose own attorney characterized him as having the intellectual capacity of "a common mailman." Eichmann's defense of his genocidal activities was that "He did his duty . . . he not only obeyed *orders* but he obeyed the *law.*"
Arendt is convinced that the bureaucracy had the power to so numb the man to his own actions that he was unable to feel the impact of what he was doing: "what for Eichmann was a job, with its daily routine, its ups and downs, was for the Jews quite literally the end of the world" (p. 137). ". . . when behind Hitler's back the Final Solution was abandoned as though the massacres had been nothing but a regrettable mistake, Eichmann was troubled by no questions of conscience. His thoughts were entirely taken up with the staggering job of organization and administration" (p. 135).
Arendt contends that The Final Solution was not so much brought on by the derangement of individuals as the normalization of atrocities: "Evil in the Third Reich had lost the quality by which most people recognize it—the quality of temptation. Many Germans . . . must have been tempted not to murder. . . . But, God knows, they learned to resist temptation."

5. John Steinbeck, *The Moon Is Down*, p. 88.

6. Arthur Laurents, *Home of the Brave*, p. 88.

7. Donald Bevan, *Stalag 17*, p. 41.

8. Moss Hart, *Winged Victory*, in *Best Plays of 1942–1943*, ed. Burns Mantle (New York: Dodd and Mead, 1943), p. 82.

9. Paul Osborn, *A Bell for Adano*, p. 15.

10. Robert Sherwood, *The Rugged Path*, p. 325.

11. Ibid., p. 328.

12. Thomas Heggen and Joshua Logan, *Mr. Roberts* (New York: Dramatists Play Service, 1948), pp. 7–8.

13. Ibid., p. 72.

14. Daniel Rodgers, *The Work Ethic in Industrial America*, p. 125.

15. Elmer Rice, *Flight to the West*, p. 241.

16. It is interesting to note that Robert Sherwood, who is perhaps best known for his satiric treatment of the absurdity of war in *Idiot's Delight*, expresses in two plays both sympathy and support for the man in search of a meaningful life through wartime heroics. Yet I find no contradiction in the compassionate portrait of Morey Vinion and the scathing satire in *Idiot's Delight*. Like the hospital patient who loves his doctor while hating the medical profession, Sherwood can see the virtues of heroism in one man without holding him responsible for the state of the world in which he achieves it.

17. Harvey Brown, *A Sound of Hunting*, p. 25.

18. In the same manner, Laurents points up the absurdity of military achievement in *Home of the Brave* (discussed earlier in the chapter). In this character study of five mapmakers who stranded a buddy in a war zone, the chaos of their lives is reenforced by the ludicrousness of the military hierarchy of the group: the lowest ranking member of the outfit is a thirty-five-year-old corporal who is a successful executive at home, and the commander of the unit is a twenty-six-year-old fresh out of officer's candidate school.

19. Robert Sherwood, *There Shall Be No Night*, p. 51.

20. Hart, *Winged Victory*, p. 34.

CHAPTER V

1. "A Matter of Hopelessness in *Death of a Salesman*: A Symposium with Arthur Miller, Richard Watts, John Beaufort, Martin Dworkin, David W. Thompson, and Phillip Gelb." In *Two Modern American Tragedies*, ed. John D. Hurrell (New York: Scribner, 1961), pp. 76–81.

2. David Riesman, *The Lonely Crowd*, p. 173.

3. Ibid., p. 140 ff. Where Riesman and Miller appear to part company is on the issue of how prevalent the outerdirected philosophy is in society in the late 1940s and early 1950s. Riesman contends that it is, and has been for some time, the central value system of modern bureaucratic American society. Miller, as *Death of a Salesman* demonstrates, sees traditional, pre-industrial work values still to be very much in evidence, although they are clouded over by the wrong-headed thinking of the world's Willy Lomans.

4. Barry Edward Gross, "Peddler and Pioneer in *Death of a Salesman*." In *Studies in "Death of a Salesman,"* pp. 29–34.

5. Arthur Miller, "On Social Plays," in Hurrell, *Two Modern American Tragedies*, p. 42.

6. Arthur Miller, *Death of a Salesman*, p. 4.

7. To a certain extent both Willy's and Miller's attitude toward carpentry dates the play. Up until the very recent housing slowdown, carpentry had become a job with a great deal of romance attached to it, owing to the skyrocketing wages in the construction industry and the value placed on "working with one's hands" by a generation of technology and liberal arts graduates. Moreover, the glamour and independence as-

Notes

sociated with sales work appear to have faded considerably in the last thirty years.

8. Miller, *Salesman*, p. 52.

9. See especially Daniel T. Rodgers, *The Work Ethic in Industrial America, 1850–1920*, chapter 3, pp. 65–93.

10. Harold Clurman, "Review of *Death of a Salesman*." In Hurrell, *Two Modern American Tragedies*, p. 66.

11. Arthur Miller, *Salesman*, p. 89.

12. Ibid., pp. 50–51.

13. Ibid., pp. 32–33.

14. Ibid., p. 42.

15. Ibid., p. 95.

16. Miller, "On Social Plays," in Hurrell, *Two Modern American Tragedies*, p. 43.

17. Eleanor Clark and others have cited Howard's firing of Willy as an example of the play's condemnation of the capitalist system, but if anything that scene condemns Willy's own value system. Howard is in effect Willy's third son—the man who "made it" by Willy's own formula. Howard gained his wealth, his position, his maid, and his love of new technological gadgetry not by work but by his family connection: the one big break that catapults a man from "nothing" to "something." When we see Howard on the job, he is not working but is playing with a new tape recorder. So enchanted is he with the idiotic taping he has made of his family that he is unaware for several minutes that Willy is not in New England. When Willy begins to plead for a job change, Howard retreats in discomfort and embarrassment only to return later to fire Willy without a pension or a salary. Howard, clearly an inept and unfeeling man who has not earned the power he holds over Willy, uses that power to destroy him.

18. Arthur Miller, *All My Sons*, p. 358.

19. Ibid., p. 420.

20. Ibid., p. 383.

21. Ibid., p. 430.

22. Ibid., p. 420.

23. Kenneth Tynan, in Hurrell, *Two Modern American Tragedies*, p. 125.

24. Tennessee Williams, *Moony's Kid Don't Cry*, pp. 8–9.

25. Ibid., p. 9.

26. Tennessee Williams, *The Glass Menagerie*, p. 439.

27. Ibid., p. 437.

28. Ibid., p. 468.

29. Ibid., p. 448.

30. Ibid., p. 481.

31. Ibid., p. 491.

32. Ibid., pp. 508–9.

33. Paddy Chayefsky, *The Mother*, in *Best Television Plays*, ed. Gore Vidal (New York: Ballantine, 1959), p. 29.

34. Paddy Chayefsky, *Middle of the Night*, p. 30.

Work and the Work Ethic

CHAPTER VI

1. Whether or not the political climate of the 1960s was the result of immediate social forces or long-term social trends is for historians to debate. However, the fact that many people during the 1960s perceived that decade to be unique and revolutionary, rather than evolutionary, added impetus to the self-consciously radical stance one sees in so much of the social and artistic activity of the period. See Theodore Roszak, *The Making of a Counter Culture* (Garden City, N.J.: Doubleday, 1969), and Charles Reich, *The Greening of America* (New York: Random House, 1970).

2. One could make the case that the later plays of Shepard, such as *The Curse of the Starving Class* (1976), deal with work themes, but even here, an analysis of the nature of work in America is fairly far removed from both Shepard's intention in his plays and his impact upon American drama. Very much concerned with the counter culture revolutions of the period, Shepard is, as Jack Gelber has said, "as American as peyote, magic mushrooms, Rock and Roll, and medicine bundles."

3. Eugene D. Genovese, *Roll Jordan Roll: The World the Slaves Made*, pp. 309–21.

4. Lawrence W. Levine, *Black Culture and Black Consciousness*, p. 143.

5. Ibid., p. 143.

6. Genovese, *Roll Jordan Roll*, p. 311.

7. Ibid., p. 322. Many observers of African and Afro-American culture have observed the contrast between African collectivism and bourgeois European individualism and have alluded to it in their discussions of various aspects of Afro-American life. See, for example, Samella Lewis, *Art African American* (New York: Harcourt and Brace, 1978) and Eileen Southern, *Music of Black Americans* (New York: Norton and Company, 1971).

8. Ibid., pp. 602–3.

9. Theodore Ward, *Our Lan'*, pp. 131, 146.

10. Ibid., p. 177.

11. Lena's conservatism is not only comprised of biblical moralizing. Her obsession with owning her own land also reflects a profound desire to freedmen to obtain their own farms, work at their own pace, and enjoy the fruits of their own labor. See Genovese, *Roll Jordan Roll*, pp. 310–11.

12. Lorraine Hansberry, *A Raisin in the Sun*, in *Contemporary Black Drama*, eds. Clinton F. Oliver and Stephanie Sills (New York: Scribner's 1971), p. 71. See Jane F. Bonin's discussion of this play in *Major Themes in Prize-Winning American Drama*, pp. 52–54.

13. Hansberry, *Raisin in the Sun*, p. 114.

14. See C. W. E. Bigsby's discussion of the "specious deus ex machina" provided by the $10,000 in his chapter on Lorraine Hansberry. *Confrontation and Commitment*, pp. 156–73.

15. Lonne Elder III, *Ceremonies in Dark Old Men* (New York: Farrar, Straus, and Giroux), p. 91.

16. Ibid., p. 81.

17. Ibid., p. 26.

18. See Levine's discussion of black heroes, especially the "Black Bandit," *Black Culture*, pp. 407–19.

19. Elder, *Ceremonies*, pp. 100–101.

20. Levine, *Black Culture*, p. 420.

21. It is generally conceded that white acceptance of black plays in the early sixties was partly responsible for the movement among militant playwrights to write plays that were offensive and/or incomprehensible to whites. The mere fact that white critics, producers, and theater owners could pass judgment on black plays was enough to drive many black theater people into their own community theaters so that they could control their own art. For a brief history and apologia of black community theater in the 1960s see Woody King and Ron Milner, "Evolution of a People's Theater," *Black Drama Anthology* (New York: Columbia University Press, 1972), pp. vii-x.

22. Ibid., p. ix.

23. Douglas Turner Ward, *Happy Ending*, p. 226.

24. Ibid., p. 242.

25. Ibid., pp. 239–40.

26. Genovese, *Roll Jordan Roll*, pp. 599–613.

27. For a discussion of militant black dramas as allegorical morality plays, see Darwin Turner's introduction to *Black Drama: An Anthology*.

28. In LeRoi Jones, *The Great Goodness of Life (A Coon Show)*, p. 142.

29. Clayton Riley, "Introduction," *A Black Quartet* (New York: New American Library, 1970), p. xxiii.

30. Archie Shepp, *Junebug Graduates Tonight*, in *Black Drama Anthology*, pp. 40–41.

31. Ibid., p. 41.

32. Ibid., pp. 46–47.

33. Herb Gardner, *A Thousand Clowns* (New York: Samuel French, 1961), p. 52.

34. Neil Simon, *Come Blow Your Horn*, in Neil Simon, *The Comedy of Neil Simon* (New York: Avon, 1971), pp. 66–67.

35. Ibid., pp. 26–29.

36. Neil Simon, *Barefoot in the Park* (New York: Random House, 1963), pp. 16–17.

37. Neil Simon, *The Prisoner of Second Avenue* (New York: Random House, 1972), p. 12.

38. Ibid., p. 13.

39. Ibid., p. 14.

40. Ibid.

41. Edward Albee, "Introduction," *American Dream* (New York: Signet, 1960), p. iii.

42. C. W. E. Bigsby, "Introduction," *Edward Albee*, ed. C. W. E. Bigsby (Englewood Cliffs, N. J.: Prentice-Hall, 1975), p. 6.

43. Edward Albee, "Which Theater Is the Absurd One," in *Discussions of Modern American Drama*, edited by Walter Meserve (Boston: Heath and Co., 1965), pp. 145–50 passim. For a full discussion of the philosophical and artistic foundations of the Absurd Theater see Martin Esslin, *The Theater of the Absurd* (New York: Anchor, 1961). The artistic

debts of Albee to the European absurdists are handled nicely by Anne Paolucci in the first chapter of *From Tension to Tonic* (Carbondale: University of Southern Illinois Press, 1972), pp. 1–13.

44. C. W. E. Bigsby, *Confrontation and Commitment*, p. xviii.

45. Edward Albee, *The Zoo Story*, pp. 391, 407.

46. Edward Albee, *Who's Afraid of Virginia Woolf*, pp. 27–28.

47. Ibid., p. 135.

48. It is important to note that while the masculine, assertive, conquering Nick represents a serious threat to George, he is not a threat to Martha. When he fails in bed with Martha, she seizes upon his vulnerability and humiliates him by making him her "houseboy" for the evening. It is a price Nick must pay in order to curry her favor. Nick's submission gives George an indirect, if temporary advantage over Nick since George knows Martha's weaknesses and Nick does not.

49. Ibid., p. 41.

50. Ibid., pp. 84–85.

51. Jane F. Bonin, *Major Themes in Prize-Winning American Drama*, p. 48.

BIBLIOGRAPHY

The bibliography does not pretend to be exhaustive. It is selective and of necessity subjective. It is intended to give a reasonably ample account of the principal fields cultivated and to identify the cultivators. As a working rule, only publications appearing between 1959 and 1979 (inclusive) are listed; however, the rule has a number of exceptions.

PLAYS

Albee, Edward. *The American Dream*. New York: Signet, 1960.
———. *Who's Afraid of Virginia Woolf?* New York: Atheneum, 1966.
———. *The Zoo Story*. In *Famous American Plays of the 1950's*, edited by Lee Strasberg, pp. 385–415. New York: Dell, 1962.
Arent, Arthur. *Power*. In *Federal Theater Plays*, edited by Pierre de Rohan, pp. 3–91. New York: Da Capo, 1975.
———. *Triple-A Plowed Under*. In *Federal Theater Plays*, edited by Pierre de Rohan, pp. 3–57. New York: Da Capo, 1975.
Atlas, Leopold. *But for the Grace of God*. New York: Samuel French, 1937.
Barry, Philip. *Holiday*. New York: Samuel French, 1929.
Bengal, Ben. *Plant in the Sun*. In *Best Short Plays of the Social Theatre*, edited by William Kozlenko, pp. 3–39. New York: Random House, 1939.
Bevan, Donald. *Stalag 17*. New York: Dramatists Play Service, 1948.
Blitzstein, Marc. *The Cradle Will Rock*. In *Best Short Plays of the Social Theatre*, edited by William Kozlenko, pp. 139–76. New York: Random House, 1939.
Brewer, George. *Tide Rising*. New York: Dramatists Play Service, 1937.
Brown, Harvey. *A Sound of Hunting*. Chicago: Dramatic Publishing, 1945.
Chayefsky, Paddy. *Middle of the Night*. New York: Random House, 1957.
Gardner, Herb. *A Thousand Clowns*. New York: Samuel French, 1961.

Jones, LeRoi. *The Great Goodness of Life*. In *A Black Quartet*. New York: New American Library, 1970.

Kaufman, George S., and Moss Hart. *Beggar on Horseback*. St. Clair Shores, Mich.: Scholarly Press, 1925.

Kingsley, Sidney. *Men in White*. New York: Samuel French, 1933.

Kozlenko, William. *The Earth Is Ours*. In *Best Short Plays of the Social Theatre*, edited by William Kozlenko, pp. 231–60. New York: Random House, 1939.

Lashing, Orrie, and Milo Hastings. *Class of '29*. New York: Samuel French, 1939.

Laurents, Arthur. *Home of the Brave*. In *Famous American Plays of the 1940's*, edited by Henry Hewes, pp. 113–97. New York: Dell, 1960.

Lawson, John Howard. *Marching Song*. New York: Dramatists Play Service, 1937.

———. *Processional*. In *Contemporary Drama*, edited by E. Bradlee Watson and Benfield Pressey, pp. 183–261. Vol. 1. New York: Scribner's, 1931.

Maltz, Albert. *Black Pit*. New York: G. P. Putnam's, 1935.

Miller, Arthur. *All My Sons*. In *Six Great Modern Plays*, pp. 355–433. New York: Dell, 1956.

———. *Death of a Salesman*. New York: Penguin, 1979.

———. *A View from the Bridge*. New York: Penguin, 1977.

Odets, Clifford. *Waiting for Lefty*. In *Three Plays*, pp. 3–52. New York: Random House, 1935.

Osborn, Paul. *A Bell for Adano*. New York: Dramatists Play Service, 1944.

O'Neill, Eugene. *The Hairy Ape*. In *Nine Plays by O'Neill*, edited by Joseph Wood Krutch, pp. 39–90. New York: Modern Library, 1932.

———. *More Stately Mansions*. Edited by Donald Gallup. New Haven, Conn.: Yale University Press, 1964.

Pratt, William. *Ten Nights in a Barroom*. In *Hiss, the Villain*, compiled by Michael Booth, pp. 145–202. New York: Blom, 1964.

Reed, Mark. *Let's Get Rich*. New York: Samuel French, 1920.

Rice, Elmer. *The Adding Machine*. In *Three Plays*, pp. 5–64. New York: Hill and Wang, 1965.

———. *Counselor-at-Law*. New York: Samuel French, 1931.

———. *Flight to the West*. In *Best Plays of 1940–41*, edited by Burns Mantle, pp. 242–73. New York: Dodd and Mead, 1941.

———. *The House on Blind Alley*. New York: Samuel French, 1932.

———. *We, the People*. In *Best Plays of 1932–33*, edited by Burns Mantle, pp. 271–310. New York: Dodd and Mead, 1933.

Richardson, Willis. *The Chip Woman's Fortune*. In *Black Drama in America: An Anthology*, edited by Darwin Turner, pp. 25–47. Greenwich, Conn.: Fawcett, 1971.

Sabine, Lillian. *The Rise of Silas Lapham*. New York: Samuel French, 1919.

Shaw, George Bernard. *Mrs. Warren's Profession*. In *Six Great Modern Plays*. New York: Dell, 1956.

Sheldon, Edward. *The Boss*. In *Representative American Dramas*, edited by Arthur Hobson Quinn, pp. 845–90. New York: Appleton-Century-Crofts, 1953.

Shepp, Archie. *Junebug Graduates Tonight*. In *Black Drama Anthology*. New York: Columbia University Press, 1972.

Sherwood, Robert. *The Rugged Path*. In *Best Plays of 1945–46*, edited by Burns Mantle, pp. 308–44. New York: Dodd and Mead, 1946.

———. *There Shall Be No Night*. In *Best Plays of 1939–40*, edited by Burns Mantle, pp. 36–75. New York: Dodd and Mead, 1940.

Simon, Neil. *Barefoot in the Park*. New York: Random House, 1963.

———. *Come Blow Your Horn*. In *The Comedy of Neil Simon*, pp. 11–102. New York: Avon, 1970.

———. *The Prisoner of Second Avenue*. New York: Random House, 1972.

Sklar, George, and Paul Peters. *Stevedore*. New York: Covici, 1931.

Steinbeck, John. *The Moon Is Down*. In *Best Plays of 1944–42*, edited by Burns Mantle, pp. 72–108. New York: Dodd and Mead, 1942.

Treadwell, Sophie. *Hope for a Harvest*. New York: French, 1939.

———. *Machinal*. In *Best Plays of 1928–29*, edited by Burns Mantle, pp. 225–51. New York: Dodd and Mead, 1929.

Ward, Douglas Turner. *Happy Ending*. In *Black Drama: An Anthology*, pp. 226–45. Columbus, Ohio: Merrill, 1970.

Ward, Theodore. *Our Lan'*. In *Black Drama: An Anthology*, edited by Darwin Turner, pp. 115–204. Greenwich, Conn.: Fawcett, 1971.

Williams, Tennessee. *The Glass Menagerie*. In *Six Great Modern Plays*, pp. 435–512. New York: Dell, 1956.

———. *Moony's Kid Don't Cry*. In *American Blues*. New York: Dramatists Play Service, 1940.

CRITICISM

Bigsby, C. W. E., ed. *Edward Albee*. Englewood Cliffs, N.J.: Prentice-Hall, 1975.

Work and the Work Ethic

Block, Haskell, and Robert Shedd, eds. *Masters of Modern Drama.* New York: Random House, 1962.

Bauland, Peter. *The Hooded Eagle: Modern German Drama on the New York Stage.* Syracuse, N.Y.: Syracuse University Press, 1968.

Brustein, Robert. *The Theater of Revolt: An Approach to Modern Drama.* New York: Atlantic Monthly Press, 1964.

Clurman, Harold. *The Fervent Years: The Story of the Group Theatre and the Thirties.* New York: Harcourt and Brace, 1945.

Flannagan, Hallie. *Arena: The History of the Federal Theater.* New York: Arno, 1940.

———. "Introduction." In *Federal Theater Plays,* edited by Pierre DeRaben. New York: Da Capo, 1975.

Gassner, John. *Theater at the Crossroads.* New York: Holt, Rinehart, and Winston, 1966.

Himelstein, Morgan Y. *Drama Was a Weapon: The Left-Wing Theatre in New York, 1929–1941.* New Brunswick, N.J.: Rutgers University Press, 1963.

Hurrell, John D., ed. *Two Modern Tragedies.* New York: Scribner's, 1961.

King, Woodie, and Ron Milner. "Evolution of a People's Theater." In *Black Drama Anthology,* edited by Woodie King and Ron Milner, pp. vii–x. New York: Columbia University Press, 1970.

Kornbluh, Joyce. *Rebel Voices: An I. W. W. Anthology.* Ann Arbor: University of Michigan Press, 1968.

Kozlenko, William. "Introduction." In *Best Short Plays of the Social Theatre,* edited by William Kozlenko, pp. vii–xi. New York: Random House, 1939.

Krutch, Joseph Wood. *American Drama Since 1918.* Rev. ed. New York: Braziller, 1957.

Meserve, Walter, ed. *Studies in "Death of a Salesman."* Columbus, Ohio: Bobbs Merrill, 1972.

Miller, Perry, and Thomas H. Johnson, eds. *The Puritans,* Vol. 1. Rev. ed. New York: Harper & Row, 1963.

Palmieri, Anthony F. R. "Elmer Rice: A Playwright's Vision of America." Ph.D. dissertation, University of Maryland, 1974.

Rice, Elmer. *The Living Theater.* Westport, Conn.: Greenwood Press, 1959.

———. *Minority Report: An Autobiography.* New York: Simon & Schuster, 1963.

Rutenberg, Michael. *Edward Albee: Playwright in Protest.* New York: D. B. S., 1969.

Bibliography

Sheaffer, Louis. *O'Neill: Son and Playwright*. Boston: Little, Brown, 1973.

Styan, John D. *The Dark Comedy: The Development of Modern Comic Tragedy*. 2d ed. Cambridge, England: Cambridge University Press, n.d.

Tawney, R. H. *Religion and the Rise of Capitalism*. Gloucester, Mass.: Peter Smith, 1962.

Turner, Darwin T. "Introduction." In *Black Drama: An Anthology*, edited by Darwin Turner, pp. iii–xv. Columbus, Ohio: Bobbs Merrill, 1970.

Weales, Gerald. *American Drama Since World War II*. New York: Harcourt and Brace, 1962.

———. *The Jumping-off Place: American Drama in the 1960's*. New York: Macmillan, 1969.

Weber, Max. *The Protestant Ethic and the Spirit of Capitalism*. Translated by Talcott Parsons. New York: Scribner's, 1958.

Wilson, Garff B. *Three Hundred Years of American Drama and Theater from "Ye Bear" and "Ye Cubb" to "Hair."* Englewood Cliffs, N.J.: Prentice-Hall, 1973.

SECONDARY SOURCES

Abramson, Doris. *Negro Playwrights in the American Theater, 1925–1959*. New York: Columbia University Press, 1967.

Albee, Edward. "Which Theater Is the Absurd One?" In *Discussions of Modern American Drama*, edited by Walter Meserve. Boston: Heath & Co., 1965.

Arendt, Hannah. *Eichmann in Jerusalem*. New York: Viking, 1963.

Bigsby, C. W. E. *Confrontation and Commitment: A Study of Contemporary American Drama, 1959–1966*. Columbia: University of Missouri Press, 1967.

Bonin, Jane F. *Major Themes in Prize-Winning American Drama*. Metuchen, N.J.: The Scarecrow Press, 1975.

Braverman, Harry. *Labor and Monopoly Capitol: The Degradation of Work in the Twentieth Century*. New York: Monthly Review Press, 1974.

Brown, John Mason. *Dramatis Personae*. New York: Viking, 1963.

Chinoy, Ely. *Automobile Workers and the American Dream*. Boston: Beacon Press, 1965.

Cohn, Ruby. *Dialogue in American Drama*. Bloomington: University of Indiana Press, 1971.

———. *Edward Albee*. Minneapolis: University of Minnesota Press, 1969.

Couch, William, Jr. "Introduction." In *New Black Playwrights*. Baton Rouge: Louisiana State University Press, 1968.

Craig, E. Quita. *Black Drama of the Federal Theater Era*. Amherst: University of Massachusetts Press, 1980.

Gelber, Jack. "Playwright as Shaman." In *Angel City, Curse of the Starving Class and Other Plays*, edited by Sam Shepard, pp. 1–4. New York: Urizen, 1980.

Genovese, Eugene D. *Roll Jordan Roll: The World the Slaves Made*. New York: Pantheon Books, 1972.

Gutman, Herbert G. *Work, Culture & Society in Industrializing America*. New York: Vintage, 1966.

Hewitt, Bernard. *Theatre USA: 1668 to 1957*. New York: McGraw Hill, 1959.

Levine, Lawrence W. *Black Culture and Black Consciousness*. New York: Oxford University Press, 1977.

Mills, C. Wright. *White Collar: The American Middle Classes*. New York: Oxford University Press, 1956.

Montgomery, David. *Workers Control in America*. New York: Cambridge University Press, 1979.

Paolucci, Anne. *From Tension to Tonic: The Plays of Edward Albee*. Carbondale: Southern Illinois University Press, 1972.

Porter, Thomas E. *Myth and Modern American Drama*. Detroit: Wayne State University Press, 1969.

Riesman, David, et al. *The Lonely Crowd*. New Haven: Yale University Press, 1950.

Rodgers, Daniel T. *The Work Ethic in Industrial America, 1850–1920*. Chicago: University of Chicago Press, 1977.

———. "Tradition, Modernity, and the American Industrial Worker: Reflection and Critique." *Journal of Interdisciplinary History* 4 (1977): 655–81.

Susman, Warren I. "The Thirties." In *The Development of an American Culture*, edited by Stanley Coben and Lorman Ratner, pp. 179–218. Englewood Cliffs, N.J.: Prentice-Hall, 1970.

Taubman, Howard. *The Making of the American Theatre*. New York: Coward-McCann, 1965.

Whitman, Willson. *Bread and Circuses: A Study of the Federal Theatre*. New York: Oxford University Press, 1937.

INDEX

Index